100 Years of American Cars

Cars

by John A. Gunnell

krause publications

700 E. State Street • Iola, WI 54990-0001
Telephone: 715/445-2214

Library of Congress Catalog Number 93-77539
ISBN: 0-87341-247-8

Printed in the United States of America

Dedication

Dedicated to the memory of "Friendly" Bob Adams, a man who bought, sold and owned many of the greatest American cars built in the past century.

Photo Sources

Many of the photos appearing in this book originally appeared in THE STANDARD CATALOG OF AMERICAN CARS series published by Krause Publications, 700 E. State Street, Iola, WI 54990. We would like to thank the following sources for help in obtaining illustrative material:

AM General Corporation; American Motors Corporation; Applegate & Applegate; Avanti Motor Cars Corporation; William L. Bailey; Blackhawk Automobile Collection; Brooks Stevens Automotive Museum; Buick Motor Division; Cadillac Motor Division; Calendar Promotions, Incorporated; Mike Carbonella; Chevrolet Motor Division; Chrysler Motors; Richie Clyne; John A. Conde; Walter Cunny; Dodge Division, Chrysler Corporation; Bruce Fagan; Ford Motor Company; Jeff Gillis; Goodyear Tire & Rubber Company; GreatRace Limited; John A. Gunnell; Harrah's Automobile Collection; Henry Ford Museum & Greenfield Village; Hurst Performance Products; Imperial Palace Auto Collection; Indianapolis Motor Speedway Corporation; James Leake; Lincoln-Mercury Division of Ford Motor Company; Motor Vehicle Manufacturers Association; National Automotive History Collection; Oldsmobile; Old Cars Weekly; Cameron Peck Collection; Pontiac Motor Division; Supercar Showdown; Vincent Ruffalo; Shelby Automobiles.

Contents

Acknowledgements 2
Contents.. 3
Foreword 4
Introduction 6
Highlights of an Automotive Century, By *Walter O. McIlvain* 7
Steam Race Promoted by Wisconsin in 1878, By *Walter E. Wray*............. 29
The Man Who Patented the Automobile, By *Richard Bauman* 35
Mr. Duryea's Automobile Was an American Original,
    By *Raymond Schuessler*.. 41
Naming of the Automobile, By *Richard J. Sagall* 49
The Odyssey of the Thomas Flyer, By Phil Cole 53
100 Years of Autos Showcased in Henry Ford Museum,
    By *John A. Gunnell* 60
Celebrating 100 Years of American Cars, By *Bob Stubenrauch* 73
1893-1902: The Decade of Dreams 85
1903-1912: Oaks From Little Acorns 107
1913-1922: Years of Fulfillment 129
1923-1932: The Jazz Age 151
1933-1942: The Designer Decade 173
1943-1952: The Brave and the Bold 195
1953-1962: The Decade of Dazzle 213
1963-1972: Wild in the Streets 235
1973-1982: The Age of Reason.. 257
1983-1993: A Parade of Progress 279

Foreword

Everyone interested in the early development of American automobiles acknowledges that J. Frank Duryea successfully drove a self-propelled vehicle down the streets of Springfield, Massachusetts on Sept. 21, 1893. This event, in fact, was duly reported by the *SPRINGFIELD EVENING UNION* the next day. A question is whether Duryea was driving America's "first" automobile.

Writer Ken Purdy used a similar question to title a chapter in his classic 1949 book *THE KINGS OF THE ROAD.* "Who invented the thing anyway?" Purdy asked. Qualifying his answer to cover "an internal combustion engine powering a roadable passenger-carrying vehicle" (and also eliminating fuels other than liquid types) Purdy credited Daimler and Benz as inventors of the first car and said, "In the matter of the very first American gasoline automobile the Duryea brothers, Charles and Frank, have the soundest claim."

Another early automotive journalist was Floyd Clymer. In his book *TREASURY OF EARLY AMERICAN AUTOMOBILES 1877-1925,* Clymer noted that the Smithsonian Institution recognized the 1893 Duryea as "the first marketable automobile in America."

Research done years after Purdy's and Clymer's writings more closely examined the beginnings of American automaking. It revealed that there had been numerous earlier experiments with self-propelled vehicles in the U.S.

One of the earliest of these experiments, if not the first, came in 1805 when Oliver Evans, of Philadlephia, Pennsylvania, built a motorized steam-powered machine to clean the city's docks. On his second attempt to operate his "dredge" on wheels, Evans met success. However, development went no further due to lack of financial backing.

Twenty-one years later, Samuel Morey, of Oxford, New Hampshire, patented a "gas and vapor" engine. Sometime during 1828 or 1829, in Philadelphia, Morey installed his power plant in a buckboard and made a test run. It successfully operated on a mixture of kerosene and alcohol.

Another American, John Ericsson, patented a "caloric engine" some 75 years before Germany's Rudolph Diesel developed a better known power plant along the same lines.

After the Civil War, the race to build a practical "auto-motive" vehicle in the United States was on. Stephen Roper's Roxbury, Massachusetts company, founded in 1860, produced a sophisticated-looking steam-powered wagon that has been dated to 1865. It had two horsepower, four wheels and a top speed of about 25 miles per hour. Several were sold.

Machinist Sephaniah Reese, of Plymouth, Pennsylvania may have been the next experimenter. He claimed a production date of 1884 for a three-wheeled car he built. However, automotive historians feel that's actually when the project started. Apparently, it was completed 13 years later. Reese built other cars to sell, but not until around 1899.

More tinkering went on across the nation. Many inventions appeared on the pages of *THE SCIENTIFIC AMERICAN* magazine. One was a four-passenger buggy built by William Morrison of Des Moines, Iowa. In the *STANDARD CATALOG OF AMERICAN CARS 1805-1942*, Beverly Rae Kimes describes it as "the first successful four-wheeled electric car in America." It was produced in 1888 or 1890. The owner of a battery company purchased it for $3,600 and demonstrated it at the World's Columbian Exposition. Later, it was entered in the *CHICAGO TIMES-HERALD* contest of 1895.

By the 1890s, the race to make a roadworthy gasoline automobile moved closer to the finish line. George T. Harris, of Baltimore, Maryland patented a steam car in 1890 and test drove it the following year. Two more efforts of 1891 were also particularly noteworthy. Businessman John W. Lambert, of Anderson, Indiana made a surrey-topped three-wheeler that was successfully tested, but failed to attract any buyers at $550. In Allentown, Pennsylvania, Henry Nadig reported driving his one-cylinder gas buggy "probably a dozen times in 1891." Unfortunately, he failed to document his work or patent the car to aid accurate dating of the vehicle, which still exists.

Charles Black, of Indianapolis, Indiana was another American automotive pioneer. Two of his cars still exist in the Indianapolis area. One has been dated to 1892 and the other to 1893. They were patterned after a neighbor's Benz and have similarities to the German vehicle.

The Milwaukee Public Museum, in Milwaukee, Wisconsin, has a car that was motoring on that city's streets by 1892 or earlier. In fact, an earlier date of 1889 has been connected to this Schloemer-Toepfer car by some. It has a one-cylinder gas engine.

With so much experimentation going on, it is easy to see why difficulty arises in selecting a specific date as the correct one for the earliest American car. Many historians share the point of view that picking the "first" is impractical. They feel that it is more appropriate to focus attention on the 100th anniversary of the United States auto industry, which will be officially marked in 1896. Interestingly, this centennial of American automaking will be dated from the first example of mass-production, which is considered to be the Duryea Motor Wagon Company's manufacture of 13 basically identical motor vehicles in Springfield, Massachusetts.

In this photographic history, we cover 100 years of American cars from 1893 to 1993 by showing pictures of a number of vehicles from each of the years. The cars have been selected to represent a "dream" collection that no one person could really amass, but which every serious collector would love to own. There are also a number of stories that touch on the history of American automobiles.

Introduction

On Sept. 22, 1893 the *SPRINGFIELD EVENING UNION* printed a report that J. Frank Duryea had successfully driven a self-propelled contraption along the streets of Springfield, Massachusetts the previous day. Frank and his brother Charles would later say that they had invented the first American car.

This book does not support or deny that claim or in way suggest that the Duryea brothers' horseless carriage should be considered the first U.S. production car. The purpose of the book is simply to take a look at a century of the American automobiles and pick out a few from each year that it would be nice to own.

Imagine what fun it would be to take those cars and put them together in one big and very interesting collection. Any automobile hobbyist would draw a great deal of pleasure from seeing how American cars have changed and improved over 100 years.

To set the mood, the book starts off with a long story that paints an overview of automotive developments spanning a century. Then come several articles reprinted from *OLD CARS WEEKLY* that capture the fascinating era of early horseless carriages.

Next the fun part. Nearly 400 photos of cars are presented to show what a "centennial collection" might look like. Below each photo, a brief sketch of the particular model's features and highlights.

Since car enthusiasts collect all types of cars for all kinds of reasons, the cars chosen for the book reflect a wide variety of makes, models and preferences. No attempt has been made to pick the most beautiful, fastest, rarest or most valuable vehicles. Some selections would fit into a list of great cars. Others may leave you scratching your head and asking why they were picked.

The book's appeal is intended to be primarily visual. The editors hope that you'll get enjoyment out of seeing how much the American car has changed over the years.

John Gunnell
May 13, 1993

Highlights of Automotive History

By Walter O. MacIlvain

The year 1986 was celebrated as the 100th anniversary of the automobile, because it was in 1886 that Karl Benz applied a gas engine to the operation of a tricycle type road vehicle. About the same time, in France, Edouard Delamare-Deboutteville obtained a patent for a carriage that ran on illuminating gas.

Even prior to development of the gas-engined auto, much groundwork had been done for road travel. Highways had been laid down. Some 2,000 years earlier, the Romans had linked one end of their Empire to the other with 53,000 miles of graded roads. Some are still in use. At the turn of the 19th century, bicycle-conscious France had constructed a network of paved roadways. Consequently, in that country, the automobile enjoyed its fastest early development.

The earliest successful motive power was steam, starting with a vehicle constructed by Nicholas Joseph Cugnot in 1769 for the French army. In the 18th and 19th centuries, many steam-powered passenger-carrying vehicles of behemoth proportions operated on French and British roads. In 1834, an American named Oliver Evans built "Oruktor Amphibolos," a steam dredge which propelled itself across Philadelphia to work in the Schuylkill River. American-built, self-propelled steam fire engines were made in Manchester, New Hampshire, by the Amoskeag Locomotive Works as early as 1867. In fact, the steam locomotive had reached a rather high state of development here, by the time the automobile began to come down American roads.

By 1887, Ransom E. Olds, of Lansing, Michigan, had operated a three-wheeled gasoline burning steamer. In that same year, Radcliffe Ward built an electric cab and Henry Ford constructed a steam tractor. The following year was when Gottlieb Daimler, who built the first motorcycle in 1895, traveled to the U.S. and made contact with William Steinway, the piano manufacturer. Steinway then announced he would introduce Daimler's products to America. In 1890, Andrew L. Riker, of the U.S., built an electric tricycle. Thomas B. Jeffery invented the clincher tire rim and Henry Nadig, of Allentown, Pennsylvania, built a gasoline-powered vehicle. John Lambert's three-wheel gas car reportedly took American voters to the polls and a successful electric vehicle was constructed by William Morrison of Des Moines, Iowa. These horseless carriages were all basically experimental prototypes.

Then, on September 22, 1893, the SPRINGFIELD EVENING UNION printed a detailed report that J. Frank Duryea had successfully driven a self-propelled contraption along the streets of Springfield, Massachusetts the previous day. Although Duryea's vehicle was not the "first" American car, the 1893 date is a convenient one from which to trace American automotive history from the initial stimulation of commercial manufacturing to the present day. This article looks at the year-by-year highlights from 1893 to 1993.

1893 - Charles and J. Franklin Duryea build and test a gasoline-driven vehicle in Springfield, Massachusetts ... John Froelich of Iowa builds first practical gasoline farm tractor ... first auto imported to U.S. is a Benz.

1894 - Duryeas build second vehicle ... Elwood Haynes and Apperson brothers try out their first car in Kokomo, Indiana ... R.E. Olds starts work on gasoline carriage, as does Charles B. King.

1895 - First auto races in America ... J.F. Duryea wins 54-mile Times Herald Contest in Chicago snow; time 8 hours 23 minutes ... Duryea Motor Wagon Co. started; begins building a lot of 25 cars of Times-Herald pattern ... Selden Patent granted, covering all essentials of a gasoline auto ... Hiram Percy Maxim's gasoline motorcycle gets him a job with Pope Manufacturing Company as "automobile expert"... New car name: Woods.

1896 - Charles B. King runs first car on streets of Detroit ... Henry Ford completes his "Quadricycle"... New American car names: Columbia and Winton.

1897 - First auto insurance policy issued to Gilbert J. Loomis on car he built himself ... Olds Motor Vehicle Company first automaker organized in Michigan ... Alexander Winton drives 707 miles in 78 hours and 45 minutes for financial backing ... The Stanley twins of Maine construct a steamer...New names: Autocar and Kelsey.

1898 - Timken tapered roller bearings patented...Adolphus Busch brings Diesel engine to America ... 15 electric Hansom cabs busy in New York City ... John Wilkinson builds four-cylinder engine for H.H. Franklin ... Cross-country tour, Los Angeles to New York, completed in 32 days by J.M. Murdock...New Names: Adams-Farwell (rotary engine), Baker, Grout and Martini.

1899 - Rollin White brings flash boiler to U.S. ... Grout has electric lights, ignition and alarm bell...Columbia Mark VIII Lot 4 has engine forward, shaft drive and wheel steering ... Stanleys sell steam business to Locomobile and Mobile ... J.W. Packard builds car. New car names: Cameron, Compound, Franklin, International, Matheson, Packard, Stearns, Studebaker, Toledo and Waltham-Orient.

1901 Grout. The Grout Brothers falsely claimed to have built America's first automobile factory in 1896. Actually, they started producing "New Home" steamers in 1901 and were making 18 cars per week by 1904. Gasoline powered models came in 1905. After William Grout's death in 1908, business dropped off. The company went out of business in 1912.

1900 - First New York auto show ... Fifth Avenue double-deck buses ordered from Electric Vehicle Company... A.L. Dyke builds mail order cars...J.B. Walker, in a Mobile steamer, climbs Pikes Peak ... Alex Winton races in Gordon-Bennett race in France, does poorly ... Columbia & Electric Vehicle Company obtains one-third interest in Selden Patent ... Knox has 1,000 steel pins in cylinder for air cooling ... New auto names: Auburn, Garford, Knox, Mack, National, Peerless, Premier, Rambler, Searchmont, Thomas, White and U.S. Long Distance.

1901 - Olds builds 475 runabouts ... A.L. Riker introduces European-type touring car to U.S. ... Charles Cotta patents four-wheel-drive ... Packard patents automatic spark advance ...Ford's racer has disc wheels ... Debutantes: Albion, C.G.V., Glide, Lozier, Mitchell, Pierce, Stevens-Duryea and Welch.

1902 - Bicycle-type wire wheels yield to wood-spoked wheels; tiller yields to steering wheel ... Chrome nickel steels are introduced ... David Buick adapts his marine engine to a car...Locomobile adopts A.L. Riker and his gasoline touring car ... Cadillac Automobile Company succeeds Henry Ford Company ... Packard patents gearshift H-slot ... American Automobile Association formed to control racing ... New makes: Apperson, Buick, Cadillac, Crawford, Cleveland, Holsman, Jackson, Marmon, Northern, Royal Tourist and Studebaker electric.

1903 - Ford Motor Company organized, stockholders include the Dodge brothers .... Cadillac follows Olds in production race, 2,000 cars built in 1903; Olds, 5,000; Rambler, 1,350; Ford 1,708 the first year ... Association of Licensed Automobile Man-

1903 Studebaker. The Studebaker Brothers of South Bend, Indiana, made a fortune selling wagons in the Civil War. During 1902, John M. Studebaker's son-in-law sold the family on the idea of building an electric car. Thomas Edison helped design the vehicle. Twenty were produced in 1902 and a small number each year through 1912. The first gas-engined Studebakers came in 1904. The Westinghouse motor used in the electrics produced nearly two horsepower, good for a 13 miles per hour top speed.

ufacturers (ALAM) is formed to handle Selden Patent ... ALAM sues Winton and Ford ... Many runabouts have rear entrance tonneau and majority have left-hand drive ... "Old Pacific" Packard crosses continent in 61 days ... New nameplates are: Alden Sampson, Columbus, Frayer-Miller, Hotchkiss, Marion, Model, Maxwell, Overland, Pullman, Pope-Hartford, Standard and Walter.

1904 - Marmon has full pressure oiling ... Locomobile uses cellular radiator ... Sturtevant has automatic transmission...Four-cylinder Packard designed by Schmidt from Mors (France) ... Glass fronts and canopy tops are extras ... Automobile costume includes goggles, veil and duster ... Studebaker adds gasoline car to its line ... R.E. Olds organizes Reo ... Ford's "999" makes a mile in 39-2/5 seconds on ice ... Heath, in Panhard, wins first Vanderbilt Cup Race averaging 52.2 miles per hour ... New marques: Atlas, Chadwick, Schacht, Stoddard-Dayton, Simplex, Sturtevant and Unic.

1905 - Stearns' wheelbase longest at 119 inches ... H.H. Buffum builds a V-8 ... Two Oldsmobiles cross continent in 44 days .... Anti-Selden patent group known as AMCMA is formed ... Cape (folding) tops are introduced ... First Glidden Tour from New York to White Mountains and return tests automobile's reliability ... National, Thomas, Franklin and Stevens-Duryea offer sixes ... Packard offers a 1-1/2 ton truck ... Northern has air brake and clutch control ... Side entrance bodies, without front doors, and right-hand drive are the order ... New brands are: Aerocar, American, American Simplex, Cartercar, Diamond T, Halladay, Kissel Kar, Moon, Rainier, Rauch & Lang and Reo.

1906 - Olds men leave to form Thomas-Detroit... Autos prove value in San Francisco earthquake and fire...Fred Marriott drives Stanley steamer 127.6 miles per hour at Ormond Beach, Florida ... Adams-Farwell has five-cylinder rotary horizontal motor ("It spins like a top" say ads) ... Olds' Double-Action model has two-cycle motor ... Detroit factories turning out 600 cars per week ... Runabouts usually have planetary gearset ... Touring cars usually employ sliding gear transmission ... New names: Bernet, De Luxe, Dorris, Dragon, Earl, Jewell, Marathon, Mora, Pennsylvania, Staver and Thomas-Detroit.

1907 - Autocar seat-over-engine truck has double-reduction gear drive (practically unchanged for next 20 years) ... American Roadster has underslung frame and springs mounted over axles ... High-wheelers popular in Western states ... Oldsmobile introduces nickel-plated brightwork ... New inventions are demountable rims and force and splash oiling systems ... Financial panic in fall marks downfall of insecure automakers ... Sport roadsters are popular; some touring cars are over seven-feet tall ... New makes: Allen-Kingston, Brush Runabout, Detroit Electric, Oakland, Palmer-Singer and Speedwell.

1908 - New York to Paris race won by Thomas Flyer ... Cadillac wins DeWar Trophy for interchangeability of parts ... W.C. Durant organizes General Motors Company around Buick ... Ford introduces Model T featuring vanadium steel forgings, left-hand drive, flywheel magneto, transverse springs ... Percy Pierce wins Glidden Trophy for fourth time ... Fisher Body Company is formed ... Flared front fenders give way to straight type with side aprons ... Robertson, in Locomobile, is first American winner of Vanderbilt Cup Race ... New autos are: Bergdoll, Black Crow, Chalmers-Detroit, Inter-State, Keeton, McLaughlin, Paterson, Pic-Pic, Regal, Sears, Selden, Simplex and Velie.

1909 - GM acquires Oakland, Cadillac, Champion spark plug, et al ... White gas car supplements steam car line ... Indianapolis Speedway opened ... Chalmers and Ford have block-cast motors ... Chalmers organizes Hudson to build a 20-horsepower runabout ... Paige-Detroit, Brush, Oakland, Stearns have engines that turn backwards ... Alice H. Ramsey is first woman to drive cross-continent ... Six-cylinder Oldsmobile Limited has 42 x 4-1/2 inch tires and double running boards ... New: Abbott-Detroit, Babcock, Cole, Croxton-Keeton, Cunningham, Davis, Empire, Enger, Everitt, E-M-F, Hudson, Hupmobile, Krit, Lexington, McFarlan, Mercer, Moyer, Michigan, Pilot, Ohio, Warren and Westcott.

1910 - Left-hand drive on Ford, Reo, Owen and Brush ... Engines have larger valves, gas and water manifolds ... a few "fore-door" bodies appear ... Some Overland models come "fully equipped" with top, windshield, speedometer, lamps and tool ... Benjamin organizes United States Motor Company ... W.C. Durant is ejected from General Motors ... White trucks appear, also American La France fire trucks ... Cars are more reliable, shaft-drive replaces chain-drive on most heavy cars ... Peerless has electric lights ... New names: Alpena, Colby, Federal, FWD, Kline Kar, Norwalk, Parry and Shaw taxicab.

1911 - Henry Ford defeats Selden Patent liberating the industry from paying royalties ... W.C. Durant sponsors Louis Chevrolet and Little Motor Company ... Fore-door open cars predominate ... Stearns adopts Knight engine ... C.F. Kettering provides Cadillac with reliable starting-lighting-ignition system for 1912 ... Demountable rims are a popular extra ... Harroun, in Marmon, wins first Indianapolis 500, uses rear view mirror, no mechanic ... King introduces cantilever rear springs to U.S. ... New: Chevrolet, King, Lenox, Nyberg, Pathfinder, RCH and Stutz.

1912 - A year of transition: gas lamps to electric lights; hand cranks to gas, air and electric starters; fours to sixes ... Everitt and Fiat have block-cast sixes and latter has U.S. plant ... United States Motor Company in receivership ... Cadillac again wins DeWar Trophy, this time for electric starter ... Walter P. Chrysler is works manager for Buick ... C.W. Nash is president of General Motors ... Hupmobile Model 32 has Budd all-steel body ... Case offers a two-door sedan ... Rainier and Welch-Detroit combined by General Motors into Marquette ... New ones: Broadway, Detroiter, Henderson, Morris, Partin-Palmer, Stewart and Tulsa.

1913 - Packard Motor Company introduces spiral axle gearing ... Abbott and Oakland get V-radiators ... Black and nickel finish is popular ... Electric lighting comes into general use along with some kind of self-starter ... Association of Licensed Automobile Manufacturers is succeeded by National Automobile Chamber of Commerce ... Stutz uses wire wheels of new triple-spoke construction ... Failure of U.S. Motor Company orphans Brush, Columbia, Sampson, Stoddard-Dayton and Courier, but Walter E. Flanders rescues Maxwell light car out of the wreckage ... Chevrolet Motor Company organizes and opens assembly plants at various locations ... Bendix push-button starter drive appears ... New makes are Allen, Brisco, Chandler, Doble, Lewis, Republic, and Saxon.

1913 Stutz Model B. Harry C. Stutz's race-bred Model B had a 425 cubic inch T-head six producing 60 horsepower. It won 25 of 30 races it was entered in. The most famous Stutz was the Bearcat speedster, one of America's earliest high-performance sports cars.

1914 - World War I halts European production ... Cadillac is successfully sued for two-speed axle by Austin ... Mercer first with Moto-Meter as standard ... Trend is to left-hand drive, streamlined bodies, one-man tops, spares at rear, electric starting and lighting ... Ford sets $5 minimum daily wage, gives $50 rebate with car purchase ... Jeffery succeeds Rambler ... Singer has horn button in center of steering wheel ... Pierce-Arrow has headlights on fenders New Dodge Brothers models have steel body and baked enamel finish ... Enter the Stewart vacuum tank ... The cyclecar craze produces many makers, few buyers ... New: Argo, Dodge Brothers, Madison, Milburn, Singer, Jeffery, and Willys-Knight (was Edwards-Knight).

1915 - Trend is to multi-cylinder engines ... Cadillac and King introduce V-8s ... Packard comes out with Twin Six (May 1915) ... White has center cowl and slanting windshield ... Rounded body and hood lines predominate ... Cantilever rear springs on the increase ... Knox truck has hydraulic rear brakes and rocking fifth wheel for trailer hauling ... Chevrolet 490 challenges Ford Model T for sales superiority ... Cadillac has dipping headlights ... New names: Bell, Biddle, Brewster, Daniels, Hollier, HAL, Monroe, Roamer, Scripps-Booth, Sun, Standard and Yellow Cab.

1916 - William C. Durant succeeds Charles W. Nash as president of General Motors ... Nash resigned to buy Thomas B. Jeffery Company ... Owens Magnetic has Entz magnetic transmission ... Marmon is all-new with sleeved aluminum engine, rigid Brush-type frame and suspension ... Fergus has rubber engine mounts ... Franklin sedans have V-windshields ... Fordson tractor is announced ... War clouds cut

Indianapolis race to 300 miles ... Kissel "All Weather" cars have two tops ... Several V-8s and V-12s disappear ... Hudson Super Six ups horsepower from 42 to 76 by counter-balancing crankshaft and raising compression ... Enger Twin Unit Twelve converts from six- to 12-cylinders at the turn of a handle ... New: Anderson, Birch, Bour-Davis, Bush, Columbia, Dixie-Flyer, Fergus, Fostoria, Harroun, Jordan, Maibohm, Moore, Murray, Ogren, Stephens, Winther and Wolverine.

1917 - Most factories engaged in war production ... Lelands leave Cadillac to make Liberty aero engines (also made by Marmon, Buick, et al) ... Staff cars by Dodge and Cadillac; ambulances by Dodge, Ford, Buick; tanks by Reo, White and King; army trucks by Locomobile (Riker), GMC, White and others ... Goodyear Tire Company's "Wingfoot Express" Packard truck makes test run from Akron to Boston on pneumatic tires ... Premier has aluminum engine ... C.H. adopts electric push-button gearshift ... Hudson Speedster is a low, four-place phaeton ... Many cloverleaf roadsters on market ... Open sedans are popular, too, but closed cars are expensive and boxy ... New are Fageol, Hanson, Holmes, Laurel, Nelson, Olympian and Pan-American.

1918 - Chevrolet, Scripps-Booth and United Motors (parts) join General Motors ... DuPont family acquires 27.6 percent of General Motors stock ... Gasless Sundays observed by many ... Jeffery name is changed to Nash ... Ethyl gasoline is developed by General Motors laboratories ... Fageol with 1.5:1 gear ratio sells for $10,000 (chassis) ... U.S. Fiat plant purchased by Duesenberg ... Francis E. Stanley is killed in motor accident ... White heavy-duty truck has double-reduction gear drive ... New names: Beggs, Douglas, Economy, Harvard, Noma, ReVere, Templar and Texan.

1919 - Postwar styling calls for high-shouldered radiator and high hood, bevel sides, straight line bodies, closely-spaced hood louvers and glass-back curtain lights ... Prices are higher due to coal and freight car shortages ... White drops passenger car lines ... Metz no longer has friction drive ... Rolls-Royce of America takes plant in Springfield, Massachusetts ... National shows are canceled ... New names: DuPont, Gardner, Leach and Meteor.

1920 - Walter P. Chrysler leaves Buick to rescue Willys-Overland and is called in to help Maxwell-Chalmers ... Edsel Ford is president of Ford Motor Company ... Four-wheel brakes progress from racetrack to Duesenberg factory along with straight-eight engine ... Harry C. Stutz introduces H.C.S. car ... Porter is 125-horsepower, overhead-cam four that outwardly resembles a Rolls-Royce ... Overland Light Four has novel Triplex spring suspension. New names: Ferris, H.C.S., Huffman, Duesenberg, Northway, Porter, Lafayette and R & V Knight (was Moline-Knight).

1921 - Ford's ex-metallurgist, C. Harold Wills, announces the Wills Sainte Claire overhead camshaft V-8 ... Rickenbacker Six is product of Captain Eddie Rickenbacker, along with Barney Everitt and Walter E. Flanders ... Premier has battery under the hood ... Essex Coach is priced only $300 higher than touring car (usually $1,000 more) ... W.C. Durant retires from General Motors the second time, starts Durant Motors, Incorporated ... . Studebaker Corporation develops nickel molybdenum steel ... Kenworthy Line-O-Eight has four-wheel brakes ... Durant features tubular backbone (muffler integrated with frame) ... New names: Ace, Checker Cab, Durant, Driggs, Fox, Handley-Knight, Kenworthy, Rickenbacker and Wills Sainte Claire.

1922 - Permanent tops on many open tourings, plus disc wheels ... Oakland has interchangeable insert bearings ... Paige brings out compact Jewett ... General Motors Building completed at Detroit ... Durant prices Star with Ford Model T and buys Locomobile and Mason Truck ... Ford buys Lincoln Motor Company ... New names: Bay State, Gray, Rubay, Salmson and Sterling-Knight.

1923 - Cole Eight is first with balloon tires (optional) ... More low-priced "coaches" at or below open car prices ... Alfred P. Sloan becomes General Motors president ... Rickenbacker has optional four-wheel brakes ... Packard trades Twin Six for new Single Eight with four-wheel brakes in July ... Ford offers $5 per week purchase plan ... Cadillac two-phase crankshaft improves balance ... Alemite pressure chassis lube announced ... Silent timing gears are made of Micarta or Textolite ... Walter P. Chrysler is president of Maxwell-Chalmers ... Oakland dashboard controls are centralized atop steering wheel ... Anderson has foot-operated light dimmer switch ... Diesel engines are tried in trucks ... New company: Rollin.

1924 - Oakland has new Duco finish ... First Chrysler six built in Chalmers plant ... General Motors completes GM Proving Grounds ... Winton discontinues car, concentrates on engines ... Ethyl gasoline enters market ... New Essex is lowest priced six at $975 ... Buick has mechanical four-wheel brakes; Chrysler has hydraulic four-wheel brakes ... Many old names disappear during a business slump ... Ford touring, without starter and demountable rims, sells for $295 ... names "Tudor" and "Fordor" describe Ford enclosed models ... New on the market: Chrysler, Delling (steam) and Paramount cab.

1925 - General Motors purchases control of Yellow Truck & Coach ... Midyear Oldsmobile has chromium-plated radiator shell ... General Motors 1-ton is first truck with four-wheel brakes ... John Hertz initiates car rental services ... Chrysler Corporation succeeds Maxwell Motor Corporation ... General Motors takes over British Vauxhall in December ... Pierce-Arrow introduces lower priced Series 80 ... Stutz Safety Eight has overhead camshaft straight eight, safety glass throughout, low frame and underslung worm-drive rear axle ... Final year of Stanley Steamer ... Ford produces 9,109 cars in one day ... New names: Astor Cab, Diana, Julian, Junior Eight and Hertz.

1926 - "Triple protection" is afforded by gas filter, air cleaner and oil filter ... Steel-bodied sedans feature narrow corner pillars ... Pontiac, new companion car to Oakland, has rubber engine mounts ... One-shot chassis lube on Packard, Chandler and Cleveland ... Henry Ford awarded doctorate by University of Michigan ... Stearns and Stutz adopt worm-drive ... Packard first with hypoid rear axle gearing late in year ... Lacquer finishes reduce painting time from several weeks to one day ... New: Erskine, Pontiac and Whippet.

1927 - The enclosed car has become the norm ... LaSalle is smaller Cadillac styled by Harley Earl ... Chrysler brings out Imperial ... A Studebaker goes 25,000 miles in less than 25,000 minutes ... Paige-Detroit becomes Graham-Paige ... Fords come in colors other than black thanks to lacquer, but still have planetary transmission ... Rickenbacker company fails ... Ford production lines shut down for six months to re-tool for new Model A ... New names: LaSalle, Twin Coach and Falcon-Knight.

1928 - Cadillac introduces synchromesh gear shifting ... Chrysler Corporation acquires Dodge Brothers and organizes Plymouth, DeSoto and Fargo (truck) branches ... Studebaker controls Pierce-Arrow ... Ford Model A has sliding gear set, shatterproof glass, four-wheel brakes, water pump and larger motor ... Oldsmobile engine good for 50,000 miles without overhaul ... Dodge retires its faithful four ... Oakland-Pontiac invents cross flow radiator ... Fuel pump is a novelty on Oldsmobiles ... New names: DeSoto, Plymouth and Fargo.

1929 - Chevrolet becomes a six ... Auto radios are new ... Roosevelt straight eight marketed by Marmon costs only $995 ... All Pierce-Arrows are now straight eights ... Cord and Ruxton front-drive cars appear ... Chrysler and Olds Viking have downdraft carburetors ... Stutz brings out smaller Blackhawk series ... Open cars have nearly disappeared, except for rumble seat roadsters and a few sport phaetons ... Franklin Pirate invents concealed running boards ... Buicks have "pregnant cow" look ... Wire wheels with drop center rims introduced. New nameplates include Blackhawk, Roosevelt and Viking.

1930 - Great Depression year ... Marquette is a smaller companion to Buick, but its design is like that of an Olds ... Austin Bantam is American version of British Austin Seven ... Cadillac offers first production 16-cylinder engine, plus a V-12, both with valve-in-head motors ... Studebaker introduces free-wheeling and muffled carburetor ... Buick has oil cooling radiator ... Stock market crash brings prices down ... General Motors takes over Opel of Germany ... New names: Austin, Graham, Marquette and Willys.

1931 - Marmon 16 has an aluminum engine with steel liners ... Great Depression results in scramble for engineering advancements to stimulate sales ... All Buicks are straight eights with synchromesh transmissions ... Plymouth's "Floating Power" brings smoothness to four-cylinder engine ... Widespread adoption of free-wheeling ... Valve seat inserts are a Chrysler innovation ... Packard has driver-adjustable shock absorbers ... Graham has aluminum cylinder head ... New name: Marmon-Herrington (4x4 truck).

1932 Oakland name is discontinued ... Ford V-8 is smallest eight ... Vacuum clutch control in General Motors and Chrysler products relieves left foot ... Visors disappear from windshields and move inside ... Style calls for clamshell lamps and sweeping fenders ... Graham introduces skirted fenders ... Hudson brings out cast-iron crankshafts ... Automatic choke on Olds and Packard ... Essex Terraplane has narrow tread ... Cadillac's headlights give four beam choices ... Chrysler products cover cowl with elongated hood ... Franklin uses cooling blower for "super-charging" ... Nash big cars have worm drive ... New nameplate: Rockne.

1933 - Oldsmobile sets streamline fashion with shrouded radiator, deep-drawn fenders and built-in trunk ... Stamped steel wheels on Olds and Willys 77 ... Accelerator starting is introduced ... Midyear Reo has "self shifter" (semi-automatic) transmission ... Chrysler transmission is silent in all speeds ... Several marques have Bendix power braking ... Fisher bodies feature draft-free ventilation with swinging quarter windows ... Many U.S. cars have skirted fenders ... Underhood radiator fillers relegate heat indicator to dash ... New names: Continental (not Lincoln).

1933 Pierce Silver Arrow. Designed by Phil Wright, this aerodynamic car was a limited-production model with a $10,000 price tag and only six were made. They were powered by a V-12 with 175 horsepower. This restored example can be seen in the Imperial Palace Auto Collection.

1934 - Knee-action year for GM and Chrysler products ... Hudson, et al ... Telescopic shocks on several cars ... Rearward sloping backs are in ... Chrysler brings out DeSoto and Chrysler Airflows with bridge truss construction, engines moved forward and tubular seat frames ... Ford introduces cast steel crankshafts ... Hudson, Hupmobile and Pierce Silver Arrow show car reflect the ultimate in streamlining, the last named having a metal roof ... Graham gets a supercharger... New name (actually revived) is Lafayette.

1935 - The year of the steel top ... Series 120 is lower-priced Packard line ... Lincoln-Zephyr has mono-body and frame construction, with V-12 power by Ford ... La Salle turns straight-eight ... Stout Scarab, with unit body/frame structure, is designed to lean-in on turns; it is a streamlined rear-engined car ... Studebaker has hydraulic hill-holder ... National auto shows are moved up to November ... Hudson "'Electric Hand" shifts gears with flick of the finger ... Antique Automobile Club of America is organized.

1936 - Reo discontinues passenger cars in September to concentrate on trucks ... Front-wheel-drive Cord revived and has disappearing headlights ... Nash offers a bed in a car ... Many bodies and engines are repositioned several inches forward with respect to wheels ... Widespread application of windshield defrosters ... Diamond T builds diesel-engined truck ... Nash and Kelvinator (refrigerator maker) merge ... Chrysler's yearly production exceeds one million ... Hudson hydraulic brakes are given a mechanical reserve system . . New names: Scarab (and in Germany, Volkswagen).

1937 - Buick and Oldsmobile offer hydraulically-shifted automatic transmissions ... Batteries are going under hoods ... Safety consciousness produces recessed dash knobs; Chrysler products have safer door handles and latches ... Auburn, Cord and Duesenberg bow out ... Packard 110 is new, small six-cylinder companion to 120 ... Labor difficulties disturb Detroit ... Ford V-8s come in 60- and 85-horsepower versions ... Studebaker has a windshield washer ... Majority of cars have independent front suspension, steel roof and hypoid rear axle gearing; many have overdrive ... U.S. economy, fresh out of depression, suffers a "recession" ... New name: American Bantam.

1938 - Chrysler drops Airflow models ... Cadillac V-16 has new side-valve 45-degree engine ... Graham has unique "shark nose" styling ... Chevrolet clutch spring is dished metal plate ... Pontiac has steering column-mounted gear shift lever ... Cadillac 60 Special is trend-setter with low roof and doors opening from the rear ... Spares are disappearing into trunk ... Oldsmobile has unique Bakelite casting centering all dials in front of driver ... Buick and Oldsmobile have coil springs all around ... The year of the "bold front" look; headlights often faired into fenders, more use of plastics in dashboards, etc. ... Nash offers conditioned-air system ... Veteran Motor Car Club of America organized ... Mercury appears as enlarged Ford with optional running boards.

1939 - General Motors cars have higher seats, more glass area ... Miniature Crosley brought out by radio maker Powel Crosley Jr. with two-cylinder engine ... Fluid Drive adopted by Chrysler products, except Plymouth; it's similar to an English Daimler device ... Terraplane is discontinued by Hudson ... A few Hupmobile Skylarks are built using ex-Cord dies ... Buick makes turn indicators optional ... Hudson introduces foam seat cushions ... Chrysler's safety type color-coded speedometer glows green, amber, red according to speed ... Pontiac taxicabs replace General or Yellow Cab models ... New name: Crosley.

1940 - Oldsmobile's optional Hydra-Matic Drive dispenses with clutch pedal ... Packard-Darrin is custom speedster ... Concealed running boards are becoming common with wider bodies ... New Lincoln-Continental features long, low hood and spare wheel outside at rear ... GM cars feature under-seat heaters ... Dodge builds army trucks ... Ford makes Pratt & Whitney radial aero engines, while Packard builds Rolls-Royce Merlin engines ... LaSalle is dropped by Cadillac ... Automobile Old Timers is founded with Fred Elliott as secretary ... Sealed-beam headlights universally adopted ... Nash introduces wraparound bumpers ... New model: Americar by Willys.

1941 - Nash 600 has unitized body/frame ... Buick offers dual compound carburetors and 14 mm. spark plugs ... Jeep military vehicles made by Willys-Overland, American Bantam and Ford ... Chrysler safety wheel rims retain tire in case of blowout ... Shortage of materials, many substitutions on account of World War II ... Buick builds plant for making Pratt & Whitney radial aircraft engines ... Car production greatly curtailed in favor of military work ... Spring brings the Packard Clipper with wider-than-tall shape and concealed running boards.

1942 - Car assembly lines shut down February 9, 1942 and civilian truck production stops March 3, 1942 ... DeSoto has concealed headlights ... National speed limit set at 40 miles per hour, but later cut to 35 miles per hour ... Willow Run, Michigan bomber plant opens in May of 1942 ... Gasoline rationing begins December 1, 1942.

1943 - No production of civilian motor vehicles ... Only war materials are manufactured by automakers ... Factory assembly lines turn out guns, bombs and torpedoes.

1944 - War materials only again ... Invader engines built by Hudson ... Studebaker turns out Amphibian Weasels, 6x6 trucks and Wright-Cyclone engines ... Nash-Kelvinator makes radial engines ... Chrysler builds tanks and anti-aircraft guns ... Packard makes PT boat engines and Rolls-Royce aero power plants ... Cadillac makes Allison engines and tanks... White and Diamond T produce armored half-track vehicles ... Ford factories contribute armored car, radial engines, gun mounts, superchargers, tanks, gliders and amphibians ... Checker tank retrievers are another wartime product ... A few light-duty civilian trucks enter manufacturing as "interim" models; officially considered prewar vehicles.

1945 - Hudson builds arsenal at Detroit ... Postwar truck production allowed to begin in September, but vehicles still have prewar look ... Car production restarts July 1, 1945.

1946 - Crosley light car has four-cylinder Taylor engine of stamped steel with copper-brazed construction ... Substitute materials still used in automaking ... Torque converters are applied to White buses ... Kaiser-Frazer lines introduced as first cars with continuous fender lines, as designed by Howard "Dutch" Darrin ... Studebaker first with postwar design styled by Raymond Loewy ... New makes: Playboy, Keller, Kaiser-Frazer, Davis (three-wheeler) and Motorette.

1947 - Studebaker features self-adjusting brakes, wraparound rear window ... Slab body trend begins ... Kaiser-Frazer Corp. succeeds Graham-Paige Motors ... Outstandingly innovative Tucker has rear air-cooled engine, perimeter frame, electronic ignition, pop-out windshield, central headlamp that turns with wheels, rubber-in-torsion suspension ... Henry Ford Sr. dies ... 89 percent of Oldsmobiles ordered with Hydra-Matic Drive ... New name: Tucker.

1948 - Buick Dynaflow is America's first passenger car torque converter ... Tubeless tires developed by Goodrich, but still experimental ... Cadillac's innovative tailfins set a trend; left one conceals gasoline filler ... Kaiser-Frazer buys Willow Run bomber plant ... In a "seller's market" very few changes in new models ... Hudson has innovative "step-down" design, monocoque, with frame members outside rear wheels ... Willys Jeepster is designed by Brooks Stevens, a throwback to phaeton style ... Chrysler pioneers nylon upholstery ... Oldsmobile has curved windshield glass.

1949 - Kettering high-compression V-8 engine introduced in Oldsmobile ... Cadillac also has efficient overhead valve V-8 ... Ford and Mercury give up transverse suspension and torque tube drive used since 1908 (on Ford) ... Both have entirely new styling with wide body, slab sides ... Lincoln goes from V-12 to V-8 ... Dodge Wayfarer marks roadster's return ... Nash Airflyte styling eliminates wheel openings front and rear ... Tucker car is squelched by Securities and Exchange Commission ... Crosley and Chrysler try disc brakes... Nash has one-piece curved windshield.

1950 - Crosley "Hot Shot" is sport roadster with cast iron block ... Nash Rambler is new compact with a very old name ... Packard Ultramatic is torque converter/planetary drive with direct drive clutch in high ... Bonded brake linings dispense with rivets, prolonging service life ... Chrysler Imperial has self-energizing hydraulic disc brakes ... Chevrolet introduces Powerglide, a five-element torque converter with planetary gears ... Nash offers seat belts as an extra ... Olds 88 wins first Mexican Road Race.

1950 Plymouth. Chrysler's new post-World War II models had box-on-box styling preferred by hat-wearing boss W.T. Keller, who liked cars with enough headroom to fit his fedora. An economical 97-horsepower flat-head six was located under the hood of these popular family cars.

1951 - More overhead valve V-8s and automatic transmissions ... Chrysler V-8 has hemi-head and new torque converter automatic ... Buick offers tinted glass ... First power steering a Chrysler extra ... Hudson Hornet dominates stock car circuit ... Korean war is responsible for more material shortages ... Nash-Healey sports car imported to U.S. from England ... White buys Sterling truck.

1952 - Allstate version of Kaiser's Henry J marketed by Sears, Roebuck & Company is first Sears car since 1912 ... Studebaker celebrates its 100th birthday since wagon-making days ... General Motor's Autronic Eye dims headlamps automatically ... Lincoln is first with ball-joint front suspension ... Aero-Willys is a newcomer with Hurricane Six F-head engine.

1953 - Hudson Jet is a compact of exceptional power ... Dodge adds V-8 engine ... 12-volt electrics appear in Chrysler Crown Imperial ... Kaiser Motors purchases Willys-Overland in April ... White buys Autocar ... Air suspension seen in General Motors motor coaches ... Chrysler purchases Briggs Manufacturing Co. (the body manufacturer who also owned LeBaron) and gets the right to use LeBaron name ... A fire at General Motors Livonia, Michigan transmission factory sends manufacturers to other sources for automatics; leads to Cadillacs with Dynaflow Drive and Pontiacs with Powerglide ... Chevrolet Corvette is America's only real sports car; a fiberglass-bodied two-seater out in late-1953 ... Studebaker hardtop is lowest American car at 56-5/16 inches overall height ... Lincoln wins Mexican Road Race ... Lincoln is first with four-way power seat adjustment ... Oldsmobile Fiesta Convertible has wrap-around windshield.

1954 - Tubeless tires adopted by Packard ... Nash-Kelvinator and Hudson merge into American Motors Corporation ... Detroit Public Library opens Automotive History

Collection ... Imperial (1955 model) introduced as separate make ... Studebaker and Packard merge ... Dodge V-8 does well in stock car racing ... Chrysler tests gas turbine Plymouth at new Chelsea, Michigan Proving Grounds ... Buick has wraparound windshield ... Chrysler has safety padded dash ... Nash Metropolitan is sub-compact built using British Austin mechanicals ... Ford brings out Thunderbird (announced in March with production start up in October) a sports-type car with two tops, open and closed ... Studebaker wins Mobilgas Economy Run.

1955 - Chrysler Corporation has all-new styling, paint and color combinations by Virgil Exner ... Chrysler 300 is high-performance sports coupe ... Rambler installs seat belts ... Packard has torsion bar suspension and ride leveler ... Kaiser cars and Aero-Willys leave automaking during year, as Kaiser-Willys decides to concentrate on building Jeeps ... Tubeless tires are here to stay ... Hudson production moved to Nash factory in Kenosha, Wisconsin. ... Lincoln reorganized as separate division of Ford Motor Company.

1956 - Lincoln-Continental Mark II has a clean design ... Hooded headlights are the rage ... Studebaker Golden Hawk is a low-slung "family sports car"... Directional signals come into universal use ... Push-button automatic shift featured on Chrysler products ... Highway Act of U.S. government approves a 41,000-mile Interstate Highway System ... Mack Trucks Incorporated absorbs Brockway and Beck... Tailfins are an outstanding feature of most cars ... All U.S. cars have 12-volt batteries.

1957 - Fuel-injection is available on Chevrolet, Pontiac and Rambler; Chrysler sells it for a short while, then recalls ... Chrysler Corporation cars have torsion bar front suspension ... Ford innovates retractable hardtop ... Reo Motors purchased by White Motor Company ... Six-way power seats are luxury extras ... 14-inch tire diameter is almost universal ... Cadillac Eldorado Brougham pioneers air suspension with automatic leveling for passenger cars ... Oldsmobile has printed circuit instrument panel ... Year of ungainly tailfins and gaudy chromium ... Imperial has curved side windows... Dual headlights are used across the board.

1958 - Thunderbird, now mono-bodied, becomes a four-seater ... Several old names become obsolete: Packard, Hudson and Nash; last two are now actually Ramblers ... Dip rust-proofing is practiced by Rambler and Chrysler ... Ford's new Edsel has push-button gear shift in steering wheel center ... Air suspension made available in cars by General Motors ... Lincoln is heaviest car with mono-built construction ... White purchases Diamond T ... Chrysler buys 25 percent of Citroen of France ... Argonaut is $17,000 hand-built giant ... Checker taxicab is available as private sedan called Superba.

1959 - Compact Lark in Studebaker line ... Edsel is dropped at end of year ... Cadillac pioneers use of Freon-12 gas in shock absorbers ... "Wide Track" Pontiac has five-inch wider tread than formerly ... Swivel front seat available on Chrysler products cars ... Continental is now a Lincoln series, along with Capri and Premiere ... Several compact cars being readied for 1960 announcement ... Dodge has diesel engined truck ... Daytona 500 is inaugurated.

1960 - Year of the compact ... Corvair is new rear-engined six by Chevrolet resembling Volkswagen in concept ... Falcon/Comet is the new Ford economy line ... Chrysler's new prize-winning Valiant is offered by Plymouth dealers ... Valiant has industry's first alternator for low-speed charging to replace generator ... Unit body/frame construction is applied to all Chrysler products except Imperial ... Glenn Pray of Tulsa, Oklahoma purchases assets of Auburn-Cord-Duesenberg and proposes to supply parts for vintage models of these marques ... Rambler wagon has side-hinged tailgate ... Thunderbird has sliding roof panel ... Chrysler innovates fiber optics for lighting dials from central source ... Chrysler introduces four-way flashers.

1961 - International-Harvester brings out Scout to rival Jeep ... Ford's Falcon-engined Econoline and Chevrolet's Corvair-engined Greenbrier are compact vans ... Pontiac's compact Tempest has flexible "spaghetti" drive shaft, slant four engine and rear transaxle ... Aluminum engine in Buick Special V-8 ... AMC Rambler offered with die-cast aluminum engine and steel cylinder liners ... Rambler has ceramic-coated muffler ... Ford extends chassis lube period to 30,000 miles ... Cadillacs are lubricated for life ... Dodge Lancer is compact version of Valiant ... DeSoto is phased out ... Tailfins and windshield "doglegs" on way out ... Ford makes rocker panels of galvanized steel to prevent rust ... Many optional high-performance engines and many four-speed "stick shifts" are available.

1962 - Emphasis is on corrosion resistance, safety, sound-proofing and comfort ... Cadillac has turn lamps on fenders ... More brakes are self-adjusting ... Cadillac and Rambler have dual master cylinder brake systems with split braking ... Two-ply tires are offered ... New 90-degree V-6 by Buick... Chrysler has aluminum "slant-six" option.. . New Chevy II has four-cylinder base engine ... Chevrolet has seven bearing six-cylinder engine ... 1962-1/2 Turbo-Jet Fire Oldsmobile is first American car with

1961 Dodge Lancer. "The best thing that ever happened to the 6-cylinder engine," said Chrysler in advertising its Economy Slant Six. This new engine, plus a new TorqueFlite automatic transmission was available in the Lancer compact that Dodge introduced for model-year 1961.

exhaust turbine (turbocharger) ... Ford uses thin-wall cylinder block casting techniques ... Chevy II innovates single-leaf rear springs ... Imperial, by Chrysler, has free-standing headlamps... Turbocharger is used in Chevrolet's Corvair Spyder.

1963 - Studebaker Avanti is Lark-based fiberglass-bodied hardtop of Loewy-Italo design ... Transistorized ignition is an available option on certain Fords and Pontiacs ... Warranties are up to 24 months on most cars ... Corvette Sting Ray has steel-framed fiberglass body and independent suspension all around ... Ford has line of heavy-duty trucks, both gas and diesel ... "Four-on-the-Floor" option offered on all American makes, except Rambler ... Rambler uses curved window glass.

1964 - Chrysler announces five-year/50,000-mile warranty on drive train ... Most compacts have become intermediate-sized ... The horsepower race is on ... Crisp styling follows the T-bird's example ... General Motors cars have reverted to perimeter frame and step-down construction ... Glenn Pray starts production of replica Cord in 4/5 original scale (his 8/10 model name is a spin-off of the Cord 810 designation) ... Chevelle is new Chevy intermediate ... Mustang is a hot new Falcon-based Ford ... Chrysler's turbine cars are being tested by selected users nationwide ... PCV (positive crankcase ventilation) valves are new and required in pollution-ridden California ... Cadillac's Twilight Sentinel turns on lights automatically ... Driver Education is popular course in U.S. schools ... Craig Breedlove sets new speed record in jet-powered tricycle, goes 407 miles per hour... Studebakers being produced in Canada only.

1965 - Year of the seven-bearing six ... Checker and Studebaker switch to Chevrolet engines ... Corvette is first to have four-wheel disc brakes ... General Motors cars get telescoping steering column ... AMC introduces sporty Marlin ... Chevy Corvair is re-engineered to use coil rear springs instead of transverse ... Seat belts become standard equipment ... Ralph Nader's book *UNSAFE AT ANY SPEED* puts crimp in Corvair sales ... Late in 1965 the Avanti Motor Corporation is formed by Nathan D. Altman in South Bend, Indiana to rescue the Avanti.

1966 - Studebaker ends production early in year ... Oldsmobile Toronado has unique front-drive system using silent chains ... Pontiac has an overhead-cam six ... More sports cars and performance packages ... Smog control package is a must for California ... Engines are bigger ... Use of plastics in instrument boards and grilles is increasing ... Windshield washers and backup lights are becoming standard ... Buick Riviera and Olds Toronado have eliminated side vent windows for better airflow ... Toothed belt camshaft drive is coming in.

1967 - Cadillac introduces front-drive Eldorado patterned on Toronado ... Mercury Cougar is new sports model, as is the Chevrolet Camaro ... Imperial is finally unitized ... Thunderbird drops unitized construction and adds a four-door ... AMC is last to discontinue torque tube drive ... Dual master brake cylinders adopted universally ... Several modifications to engines for clean air; stringent systems mandatory for California ... Government has imposed 17 new safety standards for 1968 ... Lincoln-Continental's 462 cubic inch V-8 is biggest engine ... Cadillac uses stamped rocker arms and no rocker shaft ... Disc brakes up front are optional on nearly all makes ... Disappearing windshield wipers are new.

1968 - Lane-changing indicator lamps are in ... Plastic grilles more popular; entire bumper and front end are plastic on some Pontiacs ... More concealed headlamps ... Air Injection Reactors decrease noxious emissions ... Cadillac 472 cubic inch V-8 is ahead in horsepower race ... Ford offers tailgate window washer ... Chevrolet has staggered shock absorber mounting in rear ... All have corner marker lamps ... Trend is to larger engines, higher gear ratios ...Checker becomes America's first diesel passenger car.

1968 American Motors AMX. As it became obvious that the interest in economy cars was starting to lag, AMC was forced to follow the "Big Three's" example and bring out a sports compact model. The unique AMX was a two-seater with a long list of engine options, some of which placed it in the muscle car category.

1969 - Congress enacts very strict emissions laws ... Higher horsepower/larger displacement engine trend continues ... Chrysler cars with air conditioning come without side vent windows ... Chrysler takes over Rootes Motors of Great Britain ... General Motors cars have steel beams inside doors ... Corvettes and others with disappearing headlights have built-in headlamp washers ... Corvair is discontinued.

1970 - Ford introduces Maverick and AMC introduces the Hornet and the Gremlin ... Lincoln-Continental shifts to separate body and frame . ... . General Motors radio antennas are embedded in the windshield glass ... Hurst "Four-on- the-Floor" is available in all U.S. marques ... Continental Mark III is first in America with Michelin steel-belted radials ... Steering column ignition locks are on nearly all models ... Electronic skid control is applied to Lincoln-Continental Mark III rear wheels ... Disc front brakes are optional on most cars; standard on some General Motors models ... General Motors obtains patent rights to Wankel engine.

1971 - Year of the sub-compact ... Chevrolet introduces Vega and Ford introduces the Pinto. Vega has aluminum head and block; Pinto cast iron; both have push-rod overhead valve engines ... Ford puts turbine engines into a fleet of company-owned trucks ... Makers reduce compression ratios for use with unleaded gasoline ... 17 percent of sales in U.S. go to imports ... Much sharing of basic body shells within corporate families ... National Highway Traffic and Safety Administration sets strict federal safety standards including passive restraints (air bags) for 1973; later deferred to 1974 ... General Motors goes to net horsepower ratings (measured at the flywheel with all systems in place).

1972 - Year of the profit squeeze, thinning out of some 41 domestic models ... Increased parts interchangeability ... Quality problems are acknowledged by U.S. manufacturers ... EPA dictates severe 1975-1976 emissions restrictions ... Chrysler and Pontiac electro-coat bodies for rust protection ... DeTomaso Pantera exotic sport cars sold domestically through Lincoln-Mercury dealers ... Chrysler drops convertibles (for 10 years) ... Sun roofs are in vogue ... Seat belt warning system required ... Safety recalls affect 31 million vehicles ... American Motors institutes 12,000-mile Buyer Pro-

1972 Ford Torino. For a smoother ride, the fancy Grand Torino Squire shared the 118-inch wheelbase of four-door Torino models. For the first time this year, Ford's three-way opening "Magic Doorgate" was standard equipment. It could open like a door (to either side) or fold down like a tailgate.

tection Plan ... Some Chrysler products feature electronic ignition ... General Motors uses front bumpers capable of withstanding five miles per hour barrier test on new '73 models.

1973 - Start of Arab oil embargo; 39 percent of cars sold in U.S. are compact or smaller ... Large number of recalls prompts better factory inspection methods ... New are EGR (exhaust gas recirculation) systems, five-miles-per-hour front bumpers and two-and-one-half-miles-per-hour rear bumpers ... General Motors buys 34 percent of shares in Isuzu of Japan ... Chrysler has 15 percent of Mitsubishi ... Alternate power sources are being studied ... Hardtops are disappearing; hatchbacks are coming in ... emphasis is on quiet cars ...100 percent of Chrysler products have electronic ignition.

1974 - The year of the fuel crunch ... Intensified search for alternative fuels ... Government gives grants for study of coal gasification ... Unleaded gasoline required for all new cars as of July 3, 1974 ... General Motors builds experimental twin-rotor Corvette ... Emission and safety requirements render cars 15 percent to 25 percent less fuel efficient ... Buyer preference for smaller cars catches Detroit off guard ... Ford's Mustang II is 500 pounds lighter and 12 inches shorter, inspired by president Lee Iacocca ... Seat belt interlock with starter switch is mandated to replace passive restraint law (but then rescinded in October) ... Chrysler puts four-wheel disc brakes on its Imperial ... High prices and interest rates cause death of sales, yet the United States produces a record 11,400,000 cars.

1975 - American Motors Pacer is unique wide-bodied sub-compact with 37 percent glass exterior ... New is plastic-bodied Bricklin gull-wing ... Emphasis on compacts and sub-compacts ... Severe pollution control standards dictate use of catalytic converters (exhaust after burners) ... many cars have "Mercedes-look" radiator grilles ... Cadillac announces smaller Seville (1975-1/2) ... Federal speed limit is set at 55 miles per hour ... Rectangular headlights appear on some General Motors models ... American Motors drops Ambassador ... General Motors postpones development of Wankel engine.

1976 - Chevette (Opel design) is General Motors's answer to imports, first all-metric U.S. car ... Imperial is dropped by Chrysler; Aspen and Volare are new luxury compacts ... Cadillac Eldorado is "last" convertible (for six years) ... Fuel economy is chief concern of car buyers who want re-tuned engines, revised axle ratios to save gas ... Following foreign cars' lead, few appearance changes in domestics ... International Harvester Scout has first production passenger car diesel ... Public is rebelling against big cars ... Chrysler imports Mitsubishi Colt ... Fuel injection made standard on Cadillac Seville ... General Motors mothballs rotary engine project ... Big Chryslers have Lean-Burn engines ... Oldsmobile Cutlass has the most sales.

1975 Ford Mustang Ghia Coupe. The Mustang name appeared on a new type of car in 1974. These down-sized models were not immediately popular, but gained an enthusiast following later, when a 5.0 liter V-8 was made available. The Ghia model was aimed at the sports/luxury end of the market.

1977 - Down-sizing begins in earnest, especially by General Motors ... New compact Chrysler models include LeBaron and Dodge Diplomat in luxury class ... Thunderbird adopts drive train of Ford intermediates (Granada/Monarch) ... Ford brings over sub-compact Fiesta ... Pontiac has new "Iron Duke" cast iron overhead-valve four-cylinder motor for small cars ... American Motors offers Volkswagen-licensed four in Gremlin ... Versailles is new compact Lincoln ... Chevrolet V-8 engines in some Oldsmobiles and Buicks provoke lawsuits.

1978 - This was a record year for the American automobile industry, which built 12,895,286 cars and trucks ... Ford Motor Company celebrated its 75th anniversary, but encountered controversy over exploding Pinto gas tanks ... Henry Ford II fired Lee Iacocca, who then moved over to Chrysler in November ... Firestone Tire Company was ordered to recall 7.5 million "500" steel-belted radial tires worth $200 million ... Truck sales climbed a strong 11.9 percent over the previous year ... An affiliation between American Motors and Renault was announced in March 1978 (wags joked that the company would be renamed "Franco-American Motors") ... Robert C. Stempel was appointed general manager of Pontiac and Donald H. McPherson took the same title at Buick ... This was the year of the not-so-limited-edition Corvette Indy Pace Car and the now-more-collectible "Silver Anniversary" Corvette ... Pontiac revived the Grand Am nameplate last seen in 1975 ... Most other GM cars had new grilles and taillights ... At Ford, the Fairmont replaced the Maverick and the Mustang Mach I added a T-top model ... Lincoln brough out a metallic gold "Diamond Jubilee Edition" ... Dodge introduced the Magnum XE sports intermediate ... AMC gave the Pacer a V-8 option and reissued the AMX name on a gussied-up Concord.

1979 - Death of Shah of Iran precipitates oil crisis ... Brighter quartz-halogen headlights legalized in most states ... Small spare tires are good for 3,000 miles ... Seville and Eldorado offered with diesels ... Ford's Capri (now U.S.-built) and Mustang offer turbocharger option ... Chrysler's New Yorker and Newport are smaller and 600 pounds lighter due to aluminum wheels, manifolds and bumpers ... Renault and American Motors have reciprocal sales agreement ... Peugeot buys Chrysler's European operations ... New is gull-winged DeLorean sports car with steel body on plastic frame ... American Motors Spirit replaces Gremlin ... Lincoln Versailles now Monarch-based ... General Motors's X-cars (Skylark, Omega, Phoenix, Citation) out in April; they are front-drive compacts ... Chrysler loses $1 billion ... Down-sized Toronado, Eldorado and (now front-wheel-drive) Riviera feature independent four-wheel suspension ... Lincoln-Continental Mark V is 10 inches shorter, 1,000 pounds lighter ... Chrysler 300 returns at midyear.

1980 - Poor sales year due to sticker-shock, high interest rates and skyrocketing gasoline prices ... Gasohol is on the market ... Cadillac innovates V-8-6-4 capability with micro-computer system and digital display to monitor fuel consumption, average speed, miles to destination, miles to empty, engine rpms, temperature, battery voltage and much more ... American Motors purchases Pontiac's 2.5-liter four-cylinder engine to use as option for Spirit and Concord ... Government mandates 20-miles-per-gallon fleet average to be increased to 27 miles per gallon by 1985 ... Most automatic transmissions have mechanical lock-up in high gear ... Year brings higher tire pressures, steeper windshields, spoilers front and rear, turbochargers, higher gear ratios and computerized engine controls ... Diesel options extended to Pontiac and Buick ... One year guarantee against surface rust, three years against perforation is the order ...

American Motors provides Ziebarting at the factory and aluminized exhaust system ... Lincoln-Continental Mark VI is 800 pounds lighter, with 38 percent better fuel economy ... American Motors offers four-wheel drive Eagle ... Pacer and two Concord models are dropped ... Lincoln's computerized controls include keyless entry system ... Average General Motors car has 190 pounds (five percent) plastic content ... Wind tunnel tests decree sloping bonnets and high deck lids ... Japanese observe voluntary quota on exports to United States.

1981 - Chrysler K-cars Aries and Reliant replace Aspen and Volare ... New "world cars" are Ford Escort and Mercury Lynx ... Chrysler gets fiscal bail-out from government, reinstates Imperial as $18,334 top-of-the-line rear-wheel-drive V-8 ... Fuel and anti-pollution computer for average General Motors car costs $350 ... Quality control (U.S.) is improving ... Ford re-enters racing ... General Motors imports Isuzu diesel as Chevette option ... 193,000 auto plant layoffs spur labor problems ... President Reagan institutes some deregulation, replaces passive restraint requirement for 1983 with state mandatory seat belt laws ... Changes in emission standards save manufacturers a potential $30 million ... Lowering gas prices to average $1.35 per gallon enhances sale of mid-sized cars.

1982 - Surveys show 41 percent favor mid-size cars, only 36 percent prefer subcompacts ... New General Motors X-bodies are Chevrolet Celebrity, Oldsmobile Ciera, Pontiac 6000 and Buick Century; all are front-wheel-drive cars ... All-new Lincoln-Continental is 500 pounds lighter, 13 inches shorter, based on T-bird ... First U.S.-built Honda Accord is assembled at Marysville, Ohio plant in November; it has 50 percent local content ... Chrysler negotiates with union to hold the line on wages ... Ford offers propane-powered option on Granada and Cougar ... Full-size Chryslers are gone; old model names now grace revised LeBaron variations called New Yorker, Newport and Gran Fury ... LeBaron is now a K-car with front-wheel drive and special suspension ... Chrysler convertibles scheduled for midyear ... Cloth upholstery returns ... Japanese cars claim 22 percent of American market.

1983 - End of automotive recession ... Revolutionary "1984" Corvette has backbone drive train; engine and transmission rigidly connected to rear end; swing axles; independent suspension; T-tops; and different sized tire for each wheel ... Convertibles stage a comeback ... Diesel demand declines as gas prices drop ... Recreational vehicles return in down-sized four-wheel drive Ford Bronco and Chevrolet Blazer II ... New T-Bird is an upgraded Fairmont with turbocharger and low .35 drag coefficient ... Alliance is Americanized Renault "9" (Renault now owns 45 percent American Motors) ... Carroll Shelby starts work with Dodge ... General Motors in joint venture with Japan's Toyota to build Sprint subcompact at Fremont, California assembly plant.

1984 Ford Mustang SVO Coupe. During 1980, Ford created a motorsports-oriented Special Vehicle Operations department to merchandise products to the enthusiast marketplace. Micheal Kranefus, director of Ford's European competition program, was put in charge. This explains the European flavor of the Mustang SVO, which had a top speed of 135 miles per hour.

1984 - Oil glut brings demand for larger cars ... Pontiac Fiero is innovative mid-engine sports car with bolt-on plastic body ... Oldsmobile V-6 is a tuned-port-inducted, high-performance, high-economy diesel ... More employee involvement in auto company management improves quality ... General Motors announces plans to restructure into two groups; large cars group to include Cadillac, Buick and Oldsmobile; small cars group covers Chevrolet, Pontiac and GM of Canada ... Buick's turbo V-6 gets sequential fuel-injection ... SVO Mustang by Ford Special Vehicle Operations is a world-class GT car with 2.3 liter four, turbo, intercooler and electronic boost control ... Chrysler's minivans, the Caravan and Voyager, are popular along with Dodge Daytona/Plymouth Laser sport coupes ... Federal government rescinds five-mile-per-hour bumper law ... Lincoln-Continental Mark VII has EAS (electronically-controlled air suspension) for constant-level ride and introduces flush headlights to America ... Chrysler returns to 50,000-mile, five-year warranty ... Chrysler New Yorker comes in two versions, one with front-drive in-line four; the other is rear-drive Fifth Avenue V-8 ... Escort/Lynx gets diesel option ... Use of robots increases in auto factories.

1985 - Performance cars are back with state-of-art sophistication, better handling, stiffer suspensions, wider tires, better braking ...Dodge Shelby Charger has turbocharger and electronic controls for monitoring detonation in each cylinder ... Roller tappets in many cars improve mileage by four percent ... German Ford Sierra is new Merkur in U.S ... Safety is enhanced by Cadillac's anti-lacerative windshield and General Motors' high-mount stoplights ... Upshift light on manual shift cars increases miles per gallon ... Chevrolet Astro Van has single-leaf fiberglass springs and plastic underbody spoiler ... Form-fitting seats, easily reached controls and instruments centered around the driver improve long distance driving comfort ... General Motors abandons certain diesel engines.

1986 - U.S. industry sets second consecutive all-time record with 3.5 percent boost in sales to 16.3 million vehicles ... Total car sales by dealers reaches 11.4 million (including 8,214,662 U.S.-built) despite lower forecasts ... Ford's profits are highest at $3.3 billion, versus $2.9 billion for second-place GM ... Chevrolet celebrates 75th anniversary ... GM president F. James McDonald boasts to Senate Sub-committee that company opened more plants (six) than any other automaker in recent years ... GM full-size luxury cars suffer sales decline ... Automaker becomes embroiled in public controversy with H. Ross Perot, founder of Electronic Data Systems, Corp., which GM purchased before booting Perot from board ... In August, GM introduces 7.7 percent financing incentive on leftover 1985 models ... Chrysler marks fourth consecutive year of strong earnings ... March brings announcement of Chrysler's intent to merge with American Motors Corporation ... April sees ground-breaking for new Chrysler-Mitsubishi Diamond Star joint-venture factory in Illinois... In November, Chrysler closes production of big, rear-drive Gran Fury/Diplomat/Fifth Ave. models (later revived due to public demand) ... Reagan administration continues general moratorium on new regulations affecting car-builders ... Safety becomes a sales tool ... Ford sells entire production run of 11,000 Tempo/Topaz models with driver air bags and has waiting list for more ... Ford introduces new Taurus/Sable cars to good reviews; admits mistakes in Merkur marketing plans ... Automatic seat belts popular, too.

1987 - Total domestic production of cars came to 7,081,262 vehicles which was second to Japan's total of 7,891,087 ... The Ford F-series pickup was the number one selling domestic vehicle ... *MOTOR TREND* selected the Ford Thunderbird as its "Car of the Year," giving Ford this honor two years in a row ... On September 30, Henry Ford II died of pneumonia ... Other automotive obituaries include Eugene Bordinat (designer of first Mustang); Earl "Madman" Muntz (creator of Muntz Jet sports car) and Dean Moon (inventor of the 1950s Moon disc hubcap) ... In July, work begins on GM's new Saturn factory in Spring Hill, Tennessee ... Chrysler is caught disconnecting odometers on cars used for testing that were later sold to the public ... Chrysler purchases the Italian automaker Lamborghini and American Motors Corporation, while Ford buys Aston Martin of England ... GM pays $5 billion to Ross Perot to get back 20 percent of its stock from the Texas computer systems salesman ... Due to hot sales, Ford shelves plan to drop the Mustang from production ... Oldsmobile celebrates 90th anniversary on August 21, 1987 ... In November, the solar-powered GM Sunnyracer makes 2,000-mile journey across the Australian outback ... Bob Stempel becomes the president of General Motors ... With A.J. Foyt driving, the experimental Oldsmobile Aerotech sets a closed course speed record of 257.123 miles per hour at the GM Test Center in Stockton, California ... Al Unser Sr. takes the Indy 500 with an average speed of 162.175 miles per hour to win $526,763 purse ... Bill Elliot wins the Daytona 500 with a Ford Thunderbird earning $204,150 ... Cadillac introduces the Allante luxury two-seater ... Buick builds 547 special GNX high-performance cars to commemorate the end of Grand National model production ... Dodge introduces a new Dodge Daytona Shelby Z Turbo II model.

1988 - Domestic-made cars total 7,526,334, a slight increase from 1987 ... Ford leads Detroit in profits for third year in a row, earning $4.6 billion ... GM comes in second with $3.6 billion ... Meanwhile, Chrysler makes $1.3 billion ... The last Pontiac Fiero is built on August 17, 1988, bringing the model's production since 1984 to 370,000 units ... To settle its odometer-disconnecting problem, Chrysler pays 39,500 buyers $500 each for cars they purchased that had been used in the infamous Overnight Evaluation Program ... The Buick Reatta two-seater is introduced to good reviews at the 1988 Detroit Auto Show ... The American Automobile Association announces that the fixed cost per day of operating a passenger car was $8.39, a new record high ... The U.S. continues to lead all nations in the total number of vehicle

1987 Dodge Shadow Show Car. The soon-to-be-produced Dodge Shadow convertible first appeared as a gleaming opalescent blue concept vehicle at the 1987 Chicago Auto Show. It sported 16-inch tires on sporty five-spoke wheels, fog lamps, aero headlamps and front and rear spoilers.

thefts, with over 1.4 million cars stolen in 1988 ... The classic Buick Skylark name returns on a new front-drive N-car available with a 16-valve Quad-4 engine ... Chevrolet makes a late introduction of new Corsica/Beretta models in the spring of 1988, calling them "the highest quality cars in America" ... Chrysler's hot new models are the LeBaron coupe and convertible, the latter looking very "world class" for a mere $14,000 ... Ford's Lincoln Division introduces an all-new Continental with a European flavor aimed at young buyers ... The Pontiac Grand Prix SE takes *MOTOR TREND*'s "Car of the Year" award ... General Motors design ace Bill Mitchell dies in September at the age of 76; his credits include the 1959 Cadillac, 1963 Corvette Sting Ray and 1963 Buick Riviera ... World famous automotive artist Peter Helck passes away at his New York home in April. He was 93 ... Rick Mears wins the Indy 500 with an average speed of 144.809 miles per hour ... Bobby Allison races to victory in the 1988 Daytona 500, beating his son Davey by about a car length.

1989 - For the first time in six years, automakers lost money ... Overall industry profits declined 25 percent during 1989, with combined car and truck sales counted at 14.9 million units ... Calendar year sales of U.S.-built cars register 7.0 million assemblies ... Chrysler sells 45 percent of its holdings in Mitsubishi ... GM reduces stake in Isuzu, but buys into Saab ... Employment cutbacks begin ... National Highway Transportation and Safety Administration investigates record number of safety defect claims and recalls 6.7 million vehicles during 1989 ... Federal Highway Administration reports that average car goes 10,119 miles per year; burns 507 gallons of fuel ... Cadillac Allante bows with highest-ever price tag for a U.S. car ... Chevrolet installs the 5.7-liter Corvette V-8 in its hot IROC Camaro, after several delays ... A new Laser model, promoted as "the Plymouth of the future," appears as the first fruit of the Chrysler-Mitsubishi joint-venture ... In April, Ford celebrates 25th birthday of the Mustang with an afterthought limited-edition anniversary model ... Emerson Fittipaldi wins 1989 Indy 500 and the CART/PPG Indy Car point championship ... The year's leading NASCAR pilot, Rusty Wallace, nets $1,120,090 for year

1990 - Sales of domestic cars dropped to 6,842,733 ... Dale Earnhart is top driver in 1990 NASCAR competition with $1,732,830 in winnings ... Arie Luyendyk takes the Indy 500 in a Lola-Chevrolet with a record 185.964 miles per hour race speed ... A Chrysler minivan is put in the Henry Ford Museum and company announces sale of 2.5 million minivans since 1983 ... At Bonneville Salt Flats, a GMC Syclone pickup

1990 Ford Thunderbird. A special 35th anniversary model was released this year.

hits 210.069 miles per hour ... A new tax bill places a 10 percent tax on luxury autos and doubles the gas guzzler tax on cars getting under 22.5 miles per gallon ... Chevrolet's three-cylinder Metro is the thriftiest car in the world, averaging 53 miles per gallon in city driving ... The Federal Bureau of Investigation determines that California has the highest auto theft rate of all states in 1990. The ratio there was 1,027 cars stolen for every 100,000 citizens ... Long-awaited Corvette ZR-1 finally becomes available with a $59,175 sticker price ... Chrysler debuts new Imperial with front-wheel-drive ... Also bowing is a redesigned Lincoln Town Car stressing traditional luxury car traits in a refined and modernized package ... Saturn bows October 25, 1990; sales for year are only 1,881 vehicles, but new marque ultimately gains success with popular "no-dicker" pricing and 30-day money-back return policy.

1991 - The year of the early introductions: Ford Escort/Mercury Tracer, Buick Park Avenue/Ultra, "Jelly Bean" Chevrolet Caprice and face-lifted Camaro/Firebird all bow as 1991 models before fall introductions; also delayed Chrysler Grand Touring sedan and Dodge Shadow convertible ... Mitsubishi Motor Corporation's new sports car is available through Dodge dealers as slinky-looking Stealth ... Dodge's development work on the Viper sports car makes headlines all year long ... Chrysler minivans get their first major redesign since bowing in 1983-1984 ... Explorer (two- or four-door) sports utility with bigger engine replaces Bronco ... Ford revives Crown Victoria name for exciting new model promoted as a '92 ... Buick revives Roadmaster name for 1991 wagon, with sedan following in model-year 1992.

1990 Oldsmobile Calais 4-4-2. Dusting off its old muscle car moniker, Oldsmobile gave a fitting image to this hot new Sport Coupe that sold for just $12,562. Improvements to the 2.3-liter Quad Four engine upped horsepower to 180 and made it perfectly suited for spirited driving. Zero-to-60 miles per hour took just 7.5-seconds and the power ratio of 78 horses-per-liter revealed why. Other equipment included a Getrag five-speed transmission, a plush interior and Goodyear Eagle GT+4 tires.

1991 Cadillac Allante. The General motors V-car, introduced in 1987, continued to be available as a two-seat luxury convertible or a roadster with a removable hardtop. The bodies were painted and trimmed at Pininfarina Coachbuilding, in Turin, Italy. They were then air-shipped to the Cadillac Motor Car Division assembly center in Hamtramck, Michigan for final assembly. For 1991, the prices began at $55,960.

1992 - Upheaval at GM as losses continue; in spring, outside directors make management changes and install Jack Smith as president ... Buick's new Skylark features sleek, highly-stylized exterior and choice of a four or V-6 with standard anti-lock brakes ... Cadillac restyles Eldorado and Seville; Eldo is longer, wider and high-styled, while Seville gets structural improvements ... Dodge turns heads with V-10-powered Viper and supplies Indy Pace Car excitement ... Ford revamps Taurus/Sable with longer length, stronger V-6 and high-mounted controls ... Achieva replaces Calais at Oldsmobile and has revised platform, sheet metal and engines; Oldsmobile 88 gets smoother power, anti-lock brakes, electronically-controlled transaxle and more reasonable prices ... Pontiac updates looks of Grand Am and Bonneville ... AM General

1991 Buick Reatta. This was the last year for the Reatta specialty car, which debuted as a coupe in 1989. The convertible version was added in model-year 1990, but failed to produce a favorable enough sales impact. The last of the two-seaters riding the General Motors EC series platform was put together at the Reatta Craft Center, in Lansing, Michigan, on May 10, 1991. Base price for 1991 models was $29,300.

Corporation enters market with civilian version of Gulf War hero "Humvee" go-anywhere vehicle ... GM credit card announced in September; five percent of purchases on card will go into vehicle rebate account ... 1973-1987 Chevrolet C/K pickups blamed for defective fuel tanks, but defended by GM ... GM directors oust Robert Stempel as chairman .

1993 - Ford announces intent to issue a VISA card rebate program ... Lee Iacocca retires ... Robert Eaton named chairman of Chrysler; Robert Lutz is president ... In January, Pontiac begins shipping exciting all-new Firebird to dealers, but availability of cars is limited ... NBC television news admits its report on exploding Chevrolet pickup truck gas tanks was rigged ... First quarter of year marked by revived sales and profits as U.S. economy begins to shake off recession ... Car and truck production in U.S. and Canada hits one million units eight days earlier than same level was reached in 1992 ... In mid-April, Ford, General Motors and Chrysler report profits turn-around for third-quarter of 1992 ... Lincoln's all-new Mark VIII scores high marks with industry observers ... Chevrolet launches redesigned Camaro on March 29

1992 Mustang 5.0 convertible. The price of the 1992 Mustang convertible with a small-block V-8 was $19,644 in LX trim and $20,199 with the GT package.

as fifth of 11 new products since 1992 model year began; predicts 120,000 Camaro sales ... Chrysler's popular new cab-forward LH models recommended as "Best Buys" by *CONSUMER REPORTS* ... Gerald Weigert, builder of $448,000 Vector W8 Twin Turbo luxo-performance car barricades himself inside company headquarters during battle with board of directors ... Chevrolet announces that new Camaro will pace the 77th Indianapolis 500-Mile Race on May 30.

In conclusion, it has taken 100 years of intensified technical development to bring us the cars that we drive today. At any point along the way, we might have said that the automobile had reached its apex, that it would be impossible to improve it further. However, new technologies have made that model obsolete, not by designed obsolescence, but by honestly taking advantage of the latest developments. *Vive la* Motor Car!

1993 Chrysler LeBaron GTC convertible. Standard features include bodyside and color-keyed grille moldings, sport suspension and cast aluminum road wheels.

1993 Cadillac Allante. General Motor's luxury car division announced that 1993 would be the last year for its two-place open sports car.

1993 Dodge Daytona IROC. A 3.0-liter overhead cam V-6 with multi-port-injection linked to a five-speed transaxle are standard in the IROC.

Steam Wagon Race Promoted by Wisconsin in 1878

By W.E. Wray

Most historians will tell you that the world's second auto race, and the first one held in the U.S. was the *CHICAGO TIMES-HERALD* contest. It went from Chicago to Evanston, Ill. and back and took place on Thanksgiving Day in 1895. In a sense, the historians are correct, as most of the vehicles competing in the event were early "horseless carriages." However, if we bend the rules as to what constitutes an automobile, we can point to Wisconsin's "Great Steam Wagon Race" of 1878 as the predecessor of future racing and the practical use of mechanized vehicles on the highways. It was also the first time that the motor vehicle was recognized and promoted by government.

The immediate story began with George McIntyre Marshall, machinist, mechanic, miller and Wisconsin State Representative from Adams and Wood Counties. He introduced a bill into the Wisconsin assembly in 1875. It proposed an incentive of $10,000 be offered to the inventor and builder of a cheap and economical self-propelled vehicle to replace the horse and other animals on the roads and farms of the state.

Marshall had been, for some years prior to the Civil War, a machinist and mechanic of some skill in Shelbourn, Vermont. During the latter part of the war, he was employed by a New York firm engaged in the building of two iron-clad Union boats called Monitors. After the war he moved to Big Springs, Wisconsin. There, he opened a mill and farm implement repair business. His prior experiences with steam excited his enthusiasm for its power and he soon set his mind to applying this motive agent to a road vehicle.

The plans for this vehicle survive. They show his proposed method of gaining traction by the use of steam-powered "legs" in an attempt to mechanically duplicate the movements of a horse. Marshall's diary indicates that he was unaware that this same system had been tried by some of the English steam coach builders and found wanting. Perhaps he later became aware of this, or realized the impracticality of the system, as he seems to have dropped the project before beginning construction.

Marshall turned to politics instead. His Steam on Highways bill was introduced in February 1875, largely as a result of his own thinking on the subject, but no doubt also influenced by the successful steam buggy of Rev. J. W. Carhart. This vehicle, called the Spark, was built in Racine in 1871. Briefly, the proposition was to offer

$10,000 to any citizen of Wisconsin for the "invention and production of a machine propelled by steam or other motive agent which shall be a cheap and practical substitute for the horse and other animals on the highways and farms."

The statute, as passed, required that all machines entering the contest "shall perform a journey of at least 200 miles, on common road or roads." It specified that they be capable of ascending grades of 200 feet per mile and that they must be able to reverse and turn off the road. It said they should successfully demonstrate an ability to haul loads and pull plows. The prescribed contest had a time limit of 10 days and set forth a minimum speed of five miles per hour working time. The entrants were to demonstrate an ability to perform as specified and had to be practical for general farm and road use.

A contemporary newspaper publisher and an acquaintance of Marshall's, the editor of *PECK'S SUN*, gave some insight in his March 1, 1879 issue. Peck frequently rode on a train, to and from Madison (the state capitol), with Marshall. He noted that Marshall was constantly promoting steam wagons to all within earshot. He was well liked, in spite of possessing a somewhat one-track mind (to the point of being a bit of a bore). So when the bill was introduced, it was passed by way of a favor. In all probability, the hope was that passing it would tend to silence him a little on the subject.

Apparently none of the legislators believed that anyone in the state would take the matter sufficiently serious to actually waste time on such a project, even though some of them were likely acquainted with Dr. Carhart's success. How wrong they turned out to be became rapidly apparent as inquiries poured into Madison. Peck concluded, "The whole affair graphically demonstrates the dangers of voting into public office a man with a hobby."

Governmental bodies are renowned for passing the buck, so when confusion began to mount over Marshall's bill, the legislature, at the session of 1877, appointed a commission to oversee, organize and referee the impending race and decide upon the winner. In what today seems an effort to return the problem to its source, they named Marshall as one of the commission members. Possibly, the assembly felt a little sorry for him. In the interim, he had been voted from public office; the common fate of politicians who sponsor the waste of public funds. The other commissioners named were John M. Smith of Green Bay, and D.C. Olin of Jefferson County. Marshall was subsequently voted chairman.

By the following year, six prospective participants signified they were ready and the official starting date was set for July 15, 1878. The entrants, all steam-powered, included a Mr. Baker of Madison, Dr. Karouse of Sun Prairie (owner of a vehicle called the "Wisconsin"), Anson Farrand and partners' vehicle the "Oshkosh", out of Green Bay, and E.P. Cowles of Wequiock, a town near Green Bay. There were six machines in all.

Mr. Baker's machine developed sundry mechanical delays while enroute to the Green Bay starting point. It failed to arrive.

Dr. Karouse also experienced mechanical difficulties. His machine had been built in a two-week period and assembled in two days. Road testing demonstrated that the chief problem was the sticking of the single cylinder on its center. It was withdrawn, since another cylinder could not be added in time. Information on two other entrants seems elusive. In any case, the Oshkosh and Green Bay were the only two to appear for the start.

Much was written about these two competing machines, as well as of the competition itself, in the contemporary press. They were also described in later reminiscences. All who witnessed the trials agreed that the Oshkosh was the more attractive of the two. In operation for some two years, having been built for threshing and other work, it was of balanced design and well painted. It was described as having the appearance of a steam fire engine, with a vertical coal burning boiler, equipped with flues between the rear wheels. At the boiler's bottom was a box heater, extending forward, to which the front axle was attached with a king bolt casting. To this was mounted a pivoting, wagon type axle, attached via a coil spring. On top of the heater were the two horizontal engine cylinders. The crankshaft was toward the rear, near the boiler. Drive was by flat chain from crank to a large sprocket containing differential gears, thus providing one speed forward and reverse.

Steering was controlled by a worm gear operated drum roller from which chains ran to either end of the front axle, near the wheels. All four wheels were of wood with steel tires. The front set of wheels had a four-foot diameter with a five-inch tire. The rears were four-feet eight-inches with a six-inch tire. A second set of tires could be attached to the "drivers" in modern dual fashion for off-road use. She was equipped With a trailer for fuel and water, and was described as giving a "light, jaunty appearance" at 5,900 pounds.

The Oshkosh had already shown an ability to sustain 15 miles per hour with a 70-psi head of steam. Ready for a trip of 10 miles, the weight was raised to 9,875 pounds. It was able to haul a load of 9,000 pounds and cost $2 to $6 per day to operate. Initial cost was given in one newspaper account as being $1,000, although the commissioners referred to a figure of $1,900. Her builders and owners were A.M. Farrand, designer and holder of several of the Carhart plans. J.F. Morse, in whose shop she had been built, A. Gallagher (Gallinger), and F. Shomer were also part owners. These four men acted as her crew during the contest as well.

The competitor, the Green Bay, was a larger and more powerful machine. It was built by E.P. Cowles of Wequiock, a town some 10 miles from Green Bay. Undoubtedly, Cowles had intended to enter a thoroughly tested machine he had built two years previously. However, on account of a poor logging season, he had leased it to a logging company. He built another, hurriedly, for the contest. This was of the locomotive type, having a wood-burning horizontal boiler with smokestack at front and fire box and cab at the rear. It was much like later steam traction engines. Unlike most American traction engines however, she had two cylinders and a three-speed transmission. She was also equipped with a very novel steering system; a form of Ackerman gear with beam axle and steering knuckles. One source indicated that this system may have been applied to the rear axle as well.

No complete description of this engine has come to light, as the complicated mechanism was apparently beyond the descriptive powers of the reporters of the day. Ready for the road test, she is reported to have weighed 14,225 pounds and had approximately the same pulling power, initial and maintenance costs as the Oshkosh. Due to the hurried construction her transmission gave constant trouble, but when all was in working order, she could make upwards of 25 miles per hour. Most who commented on her appearance were of the opinion that the mechanics were overly complicated. She was clumsy (at least in design) and had an unfinished look, although she was obviously solidly and durably constructed.

Monday, July 15, 1878 was a hot day in Green Bay. For the previous few days, temperatures had ranged between 98- and 102-degrees in the shade. The race day was no different. There was a holiday spirit like circus day in the air, however, and all talk seemed centered on the start next day. The Oshkosh arrived on the morning freight and was put to driving around town immediately. About 4 p.m., the Green Bay steamed in from Mr. Cowles farm and put in an appearance on the city streets. It attracted a good-sized crowd in the process. Neither of the out-of-town commissioners arrived until later in the evening.

The Oshkosh was the winner of the 1878 steam wagon race in Wisconsin. The accuracy of this illustration cannot be vouched for, as the original source of the artwork is unknown.

Tuesday, July 16, was no cooler, but not even the heat could prevent huge crowds from gathering to watch the start. The Oshkosh steamed around the city for an hour prior to the official time, then crossed the Main Street Bridge to the corner of Broadway and Dousman, the official starting line in Fort Howard.

Though the Green Bay had apparently passed her early road testing satisfactorily, her troubles began on this morning, when she broke through a Main St. culvert on her way to the start. The shock jarred the delicate machinery and broke the governor, but damage was slight and was repaired quickly.

By prior arrangement the 11 a.m. start saw the Oshkosh start south on the river's west bank, while the Green Bay kept to the east shore. Planning to meet at DePere for dinner, they were intending to converge on the west bank and proceed in company, in-so-far as possible, along the Central & Northwestern Railroad's right of way to Oshkosh, then on to Fond du Lac, Waupun, Watertown, and Fort Atkinson to Janesville. There, they would go south to Beloit and, from there, north to Madison.

Each machine was permitted to pick its own route between the various communities along the way. Possibly this was done so that adequate bridges could be found. The Green Bay's experience with the culvert was seen as an indicator of possible troubles ahead for both, as the bridges had been designed only for regular wagons. No further mention of this was given in the press coverage, so apparently it had been an unnecessary fear.

Things began to go wrong for the Green Bay almost immediately. She had barely cleared the city limits when an injector broke and had to be replaced by a steam pump. This took the rest of the day. So before she even got started, the machine was half a day behind. The Oshkosh, meanwhile, received a spirited greeting at DePere. After a community sponsored dinner, it had pushed off again for Appleton, which was reached in about four hours running time. There she spent the night.

The next morning, the Oshkosh started out again while repairs to the Green Bay were being completed. As a result, the latter machine had barely reached DePere when the Oshkosh rolled into her home city. She had sustained a speed of nearly 20 miles per hour over part of the route. The commissioners, who followed the Oshkosh in a buggy, telegraphed Cowles. They ordered him to ship the Green Bay by rail, in order to make a real contest of the demonstrations scheduled in Oshkosh. After complaining for the record, he complied and further adjustments were performed after her arrival Thursday evening.

Saturday, July 20 saw the speed and hauling tests in Oshkosh. First held were speed trials at the fairgrounds racetrack, where the Oshkosh performed at a rate of one mile in four minutes forty-one seconds (13.6 miles per hour), with 130 psi. With 110 psi, the Green Bay trimmed one minute off the time, including a short stop to tend to an overheated bearing (17.6 miles per hour).

The hauling tests were conducted next at Foster & Jones' mill, where four horses were required to haul a heavy wagon, loaded with 3,000 board-feet of green lumber, into position. The Green Bay was hooked on first and Mr. Cowles invited the bystanders to climb on and have a ride. He then proceeded to pull them around town without difficulty. When the Oshkosh was hitched on, she was able to move the load successfully on smooth and level surfaces, but required the help of the passengers to negotiate less favorable stretches.

Back on the road again, the Oshkosh soon took the lead, as the Green Bay continued to have difficulties with her gears and bearings. Just outside of Fond du Lac, the Oshkosh experienced a tight front wheel bearing and was delayed a half-hour for repairs. This appears to have been her only mechanical trouble on the entire 200-mile run. When the Green Bay broke down again near Fond du Lac, the commissioners ordered her to again be shipped by rail in order to catch up.

While its competitor was in transit, the Oshkosh gave a solo demonstration of her plowing abilities on commission member Olin's farm. Upon arrival in Fort Atkinson, several wagons were hitched on. Then 72 men climbed aboard and were hauled several miles into the country. Here several acres of tough prairie sod were successfully plowed with single and gang plows before a crowd of some 500 curious onlookers.

Having successfully completed this phase of the contest, the Oshkosh again waited for her competition to catch up. Cowles had so much trouble with high speed that he was now driving in second. This put the pace at somewhat less than that of the Oshkosh, which was several times ordered to wait. Orders were finally received to continue to Madison. The Oshkosh arrived triumphantly in Madison on the afternoon of Tuesday, July 23.

Official running time was 33 hours and 27 minutes or an average road speed of six miles per hour, one better than specified. During the run, she consumed 4,500 pounds of coal and 12-gallons of oil. In celebration, several wagons were hitched on and the Governor, Secretary of State, Secretary of the Treasury, and the entire state assembly climbed aboard for a victory parade around the Capitol Building.

Obviously, the Oshkosh had presented a superior performance and, in fact, was the only finisher. Some 20 miles from Madison the Green Bay broke down for the last time and was shipped home. We must admire the spirit and determination shown by Mr. Cowles in his efforts with an unperfected machine. Unforeseen circumstances prevented him making a better showing with what was obviously the faster and more powerful entry.

The Oshkosh's victory was somewhat undermined when a split of opinion developed as to the awarding of the prize money. Marshall and a few others believed that the Oshkosh's owners deserved the prize, while the Governor and many others held that she did not live up totally to the provisions, in that any vehicle costing in the vicinity of $2,000 and costing $2 to $6 daily to operate could not be regarded as being "cheap and economical." Therefore the matter was postponed to the next legislative session, when it was voted to award half the prize.

As previously stated, one must bend the rules defining an automobile slightly to include the Oshkosh and the Green Bay as cars. Yet, the nucleus of the private motor vehicle was certainly in evidence, as well as the goal of an all-purpose vehicle, which we have not as yet achieved. Other vehicles no more suited to the automobile definition appear in every roster of marques and certainly, most of them were capable of no better performance. In fact, many years were to pass before speeds and endurance were to match those on Wisconsin's roads in 1878.

Nicknamed "The Spark," this steam-powered vehicle was made in 1871 by Dr. J.W. Carhart of Racine, Wis. and helped inspire Wisconsin's Steam on Highways bill introduced into the state legislature in 1875.

Wisconsin: Auto Capital of the Midwest

Wisconsin's contributions to the history of American cars did not begin with the Green Bay-to-Madison steam car race of 1878. The Badger State's earliest links to the automobile date back to at least 1871, when motor vehicles were still in an early experimental stage. They continued into the production era and lasted many years thereafter.

It was in 1871 that Dr. J.W. Carhart, of Racine, built a steam-powered machine that Floyd Clymer said, "looked suspiciously like the wedding of a buggy and a potbellied stove." Today this vehicle ... The Spark ... serves as the symbol of the Wisconsin Chapter of the Society of Automotive Historians. This group has researched cars and trucks built in Wisconsin, resulting in a list of more than 100 nameplates.

In the pioneer days of auto manufacturing, Milwaukee was among several cities located in the Midwest that had a shot at becoming the center of the new industry. Others included Cleveland, Ohio, Indianapolis, Indiana and Detroit, Michigan.

Detroit won of course, but Milwaukee put in a strong bid thanks to its industrial base, its hard-working residents and its location on the Great Lakes. And before its Eastern neighbor became the clear winner, Wisconsin achieved many important automotive milestones.

Dr. Carhart's steamer, according to some, has a serious claim as the first successful steam car driven on American roads. Other Wisconsinites insist that the first practical gasoline-powered buggy in the nation was the Schloemer-Toepfer car that still resides in the Milwaukee Public Museum. According to an article in the *MILWAUKEE JOURNAL* of November 14, 1985, this buggy "was motoring on Milwaukee streets in 1892 or earlier, perhaps even in 1889."

Car enthusiasts in the state also insist that the first sale of an automobile took place in Wisconsin. This is traced to 1895, when A.W. Ballard, a bicycle repairman from the city of Oshkosh, built a machine for a doctor living about three hours to the north in Wausau.

Rambler, Jeffery, Pennington, Kissel Kar, Monarch, Merkel, Badger, Vixen, FWD, Oshkosh, Stoughton, Kunz, Pierce-Racine, Mitchell and Case are among the long list of automakers that produced in Wisconsin. Nash/American Motors and Chevrolet (Janesville factory) are the three largest automakers the state has seen. Clymer noted that over four million automotive vehicles had been built in Wisconsin by 1950. Surely, that many again were made there before Chrysler's purchase of American Motors Corporation.

Current production activities include FWD trucks and Seagrave fire trucks in Clintonville; Oshkosh trucks in Oshkosh; Pierce fire trucks in Appleton; Excaliburs in Milwaukee; several Duesenberg IIs per year in Elroy; and Chevrolet products (notably Suburbans) in Janesville.

With such interest in automotive ventures, it's no wonder that the first automobile race in the world was held there, with official backing from the state legislature.

The Man Who Patented the Auto

By Richard Bauman

Ask a couple of dozen persons who they think invented the automobile and most will probably say it was either Ford or Duryea. A few might say it was Daimler or Benz. It's doubtful that more than one person will say it was George B. Selden.

Nevertheless, if we recognize as the inventor of a machine or device the person who receives a patent for it, then Selden is unquestionably the inventor of the automobile. In 1895, U.S. Patent No. 549,160 was issued to Selden for a machine he called a "road-locomotive" and described, in part as, "light in weight, easy to control and possessed of sufficient power to overcome any ordinary incline."

Why then is Selden's name not associated with the automobile the way Ford, Duryea and others are? Possibly because he sold the patent rights to the automobile, rather than manufacture cars himself. Another factor could be a nasty, nine-year-long court battle which brought Ford's name to the attention of the American public in the role of a "little guy" fighting for his rights against "big business."

Selden became intrigued with the idea of a self-powered carriage about 1864. This was when he was an infantryman in the Union Army during the Civil War. After the war he entered college, but instead of studying engineering he concentrated on law. He graduated from Yale University. By the mid-1870s he had started experimenting with steam-powered vehicles, but became disenchanted with steam and turned his attention to internal combustion engines.

While Selden's efforts in this area weren't entirely original, he nevertheless did develop a three-cylinder engine based on the principle of the Brayton two-cycle engine that had been invented a few years earlier by George Brayton. By May 1879, Selden felt he'd perfected his engine to the point that it, coupled with a carriage of his design, should be patented as what he called a road-locomotive.

Selden was no fool. As a lawyer he knew the workings of the patent laws and further realized that he didn't want his patent issued too soon. He intended to make some money from his road-locomotive. To do so, he had to build cars. This would require money he didn't have. Selden knew it would take some time to find financial backing for his road-locomotive, so delaying the patent was necessary. It's unlikely, however, that he expected his search for a backer to take very long. The concept of the automobile was growing in popularity and it seemed like it would be simple to find financing. However, most backers were interested in electric-powered cars, rather than noisy and balky, gasoline-powered vehicles.

Although he had first applied for it in 1879, Selden managed to hold up the granting of his patent for nearly 16 years through a series of perfectly legal delays. However, as the auto industry began developing in Europe and the U.S., Selden saw trouble coming if he didn't get his patent issued, regardless of the lack of money. Finally, in 1895 he satisfactorily answered all patent office questions and, on November 5, received his patent.

Though the "house numbers" on the side show the 1877 date of the first automobile design done by George Baldwin Selden, this vehicle was not built until after the court battle began. It survives in the Henry Ford Museum.

Frustrated, short of funds, and desperate to make some money on his invention, Selden signed a contract with Columbia and Electric Vehicle Company of Hartford, Connecticut. He sold the rights to the patent for $10,000 cash and a royalty on every car sold under his patent. The signing date was November 4, 1899, almost four years after his patent had been issued.

According to Mitchell Wilson's book *AMERICAN SCIENCE AND INDUSTRY*, "Selden's patent was the first one on record anyplace that was a combination of an internal combustion engine with a carriage."

Once Columbia and Electric Vehicle Company obtained the patent rights to the automobile, they became very serious about protecting their property. A year earlier, Alexander Winton of Cleveland, Ohio had manufactured and sold an automobile. Not knowing a patent existed, Winton was stunned when the Columbia and Electric Vehicle Company hit him with a lawsuit for patent infringement. There was a minor court skirmish and Selden's patent was sustained, setting a precedent and serving as warning to all other manufacturers that they were subject to being sued, too.

The Association of Licensed Automobile Manufacturers (ALAM) was formed shortly thereafter, with ALAM agreeing to pay 1-1/4 percent of the retail price of each car they sold to Columbia and Electric Vehicle Company as a royalty. Of this, Selden was to receive 10 percent.

Enter Henry Ford. He applied for membership to ALAM. Had he been accepted right off, chances are good that Selden and Columbia and Electric Vehicle Company would have collected royalties on Ford sales for about a 12 years. With Ford's ultimate success, the royalties would probably have been over a million dollars.

Unfortunately, the directors of ALAM reviewed Ford's application and decided he was merely an assembler, rather than a builder, of cars. Ford didn't appreciate their assessment of his company and decided to continue to build cars regardless of ALAM's approval or Selden's patent.

As more and more Ford cars appeared on the roads of America the members of ALAM decided to reconsider Ford's application and invited him to join. When Ford and his partner James Couzens met with Fred L. Smith, the president of Oldsmobile, Smith suggested Ford should join ALAM. Couzens reportedly told Smith, "Selden can take his patent and go to hell."

With those few words, war was declared between Ford Motor Car Company and ALAM. Smith was more than slightly stunned by Couzens' reply and is supposed to have said, "The Selden crowd can put you out of business and they will." Ford's reply was just as straight forward: "Let them try."

Couzens wasted no time in making Ford Motor Car Company's position clear to the automobile industry. In a letter to the *CYCLE AND AUTOMOBILE TRADE JOURNAL* he declared, "We intend to manufacture and sell all the gasoline automobiles ... we can. We regard the Selden patent covering the monopoly of such machines ... unwarranted. We do not, therefore, propose to respect any such claims."

On October 21, 1903 suit was filed against Ford by ALAM in the name of George Selden and Columbia and Electric Vehicle Company. It turned out to be one of the longest running legal wars in the history of the United States. In fact, when it was all over, the testimony was so lengthy and exacting that it filled 23,000 pages in 36 volumes.

Each side presented its witnesses. Testimony that went into the most infinite details was extracted by the shrewd lawyers on both sides. There were hundreds of challenges and counter-challenges, but through it, according to Mitchell Wilson, the American public got the picture of Ford as an underdog. "It was good policy for Ford to appear as the underdog in the fight of the little fellow versus big business," notes Wilson. "After all, the public and the press almost always sympathize with the fellow who looks like he's getting kicked around by the big guys."

When the case began in 1903, Ford as the little guy was probably an accurate picture. However, as the case dragged on and years passed, Ford kept building cars and

This photo shows George B. Selden in his road-locomotive, with Henry R. Selden nearby. Historians have proved that portions of this photo were "doctored." A second Selden built during the court case survives at the Connecticut State Library in Hartford.

selling them. He was making lots of money and paying no royalties. At the same time, as the case moved along at a snail's pace, members of ALAM became disenchanted. They began to rebel against having to pay royalties.

Henry Joy, the president of Packard, felt if Ford could sell cars and not be a member of ALAM, then why should Packard or any other manufacturer pay royalties? He reportedly told the press: "There's no excuse for such a tax (the royalties) ... perhaps ALAM is less of a help than a burden to us." W.C. Durant, president of General Motors seemed to agree and GM began withholding royalty payments too.

The Selden Motor Vehicle Company, of Rochester, New York, was incorporated during the court case and started producing cars during 1907. However, models like this 1910 touring weren't designed by George B. Selden.

By mid-1909, all that could be said by either side in the lawsuit had been said over and over. A few months later, in September, Judge Charles Hough rendered his decision. There was temporary joy at Columbia and Electric Vehicle Company and momentary despair at Ford. Hough said Selden's patent was valid and had been infringed.

Actually, the decision was more discouraging to the fallen away members of ALAM and other car manufacturers, than it was to Ford. Those members who had dropped out were back, with checks in hand, to pay past due royalties. Other manufacturers eagerly signed on the dotted line, agreeing to pay royalties on the cars they'd already sold. Everybody joined except Ford. He appealed the decision. As the legal process began again, Ford continued to build cars.

Ford lawyers took a different approach during the appeal than in the original case. They showed that Selden's carriage for the road-locomotive was not especially unique. Steering mechanisms, such as the one he used, were an old design. So were clutches, gears and other parts Selden had incorporated into his patent.

When Ford's lawyers started talking engines, they really struck pay dirt. Basically, there were two types of engines before Selden created his three-cylinder power plant. One version was the Otto engine, a four-cycle type. The other was the Brayton or two-cycle constant pressure type. And as far as Ford's lawyers were concerned, it was only the Brayton type engine Selden had intended to use on his or any other car.

Selden's diaries were introduced as evidence to support the contention that the Brayton engine was Selden's choice. One apparently harmless entry may have been the turning point in the case. After having seen the Otto engine demonstrated, Selden had written: "This is just another of those damned Dutch engines."

Ford's lawyers were generous after that. They agreed that Selden had substantially improved the Brayton engine. They conceded he had a valid patent for the Brayton-type engine. It was then pointed out to the court that not one Ford car, in fact, not one car built in the U.S., ever had a Brayton engine of any design. All cars built here had used Otto-type engines.

Judge Noyes heard the appeal and ruled, in late 1911, that Selden had a valid patent. However, he added that Ford and other manufacturers using Otto-type engines had not infringed the patent. The royalties to Selden and Columbia Electric Car Company stopped. Ford was viewed by his colleagues as a hero.

Perhaps he was a hero. After all, Henry Ford had fought for what he thought was right even if he was forced to by the snobbery of ALAM members. He had faced probable financial ruin if he lost the case, but he won. His victory changed the auto industry in the process.

Selden's reward for his decades of experimenting and struggle was minimal financial return on his invention. On the other hand, he did what no one else apparently had thought to do; he patented the automobile. Regardless of court rulings, that claim to fame could not be denied him.

A drawing of Selden's road-locomotive showing the patent number. Also appearing is the date November 5, 1895, on which the patent was issued.

1909 Selden Model 29 Roadster. Sold for $2,000 or $2,137 with a cape top.

1911 Selden Model 40-R Varsity Roadster. It was $2,500 with full equipment.

1908 Selden Touring Car. E.T. Birdsall designed production automobiles built under the Selden name in a Rochester, New York factory. This company was formed in 1907. The Model 29 was the company's second model.

1925 Selden 1-1/4-ton stake bed. Selden Motor Vehicle Company began producing commercial vehicles around 1913 and stopped building cars a year later. After George B. Selden died in 1923, the manufacture of trucks continued.

Mr. Duryea's Automobile Was an American Original

By Raymond Schuessler

The first automobile built in America that actually locomoted under its own gasoline power for a good distance ... in fact good enough to win a 52-mile race over two German Benz cars ... was built by Charles and (mostly) Frank Duryea.

Both Duryeas grew up as bicycle mechanics. When they left their Peoria, Illinois farm and went to Washington D.C., they worked in the bicycle shop of H.S. Owen. Here Charles spent a lot of time reading the *PATENT OFFICE GAZETTE* where all the new-fangled self-propelled gadgets were recorded with drawings.

In 1889, the Duryeas decided to move to Chicopee, Massachusetts, a northern suburb of Springfield. There, Charles opened a bicycle shop. Frank hired out as a tool-maker with the Ames Company.

Having spare time on his hands, Charles began to study several books on gasoline engines. He coupled this with his reading at the U.S. Patent Office and wondered if he could build an automobile like the Europeans had.

There were bugs in all the cars ever invented he knew, but surely good mechanics and designers could overcome any problem. The Europeans already had a pretty good horseless carriage on the road. Why not try to build an American automobile?

When Charles Duryea visited Hartford, Connecticut on business, he stopped at the Hartford Machine Screw Company where a Daimler-type engine was being made. Examining the engine, he found it a ponderous and clumsy contraption.

He then visited the Pope Manufacturing Company the makers of the Columbia bicycle. Talking to their engineers, he got a tip on a sort of "free piston." He became more determined than ever to build an experimental model.

Duryea made extensive studies of the German Benz blueprints. A model of his first car shows evidence of this. Charles reversed the engine so the flywheel was to the front rather than the rear. This eliminated the need for a long drive belt that the Benz used.

His original plan included Benz-like details of the axles, steering gear, counter-shaft (with its friction drum) and a two-piece, angle iron frame upon which the countershaft bearings were mounted.

No provision was made for a burner to heat the hot tube ignition, nor had a carburetor been designed. The plan called for no muffler or starting arrangement. Like most engines of that time, Duryea's started by turning the flywheel by hand.

Charles E. Duryea, in about 1894, as drawn by George Giguere from a photograph (Smithsonian Institution)

Since the Ames Company plant shut down for the month of August 1891, the Duryea brothers had access to the empty plant to carry on their experiments. They worked mostly on blueprints.

In January 1892, Duryea needed financing for a place to work, a mechanic to do the work and a carriage to hold his invention. He found an old used "ladies' phaeton," which he bought for $70. His financial backer was Erwin F. Markham, of Springfield, who put up $1,000 in return for a five-tenths share of the business.

If the money was depleted, Mr. Markham would have the option to continue helping until a successful car was built and keep his half share or to refuse investing additional money and give up four of his five-tenths interest.

On March 28, space was found at the John W. Russell & Sons Company in Springfield. This company had just completed a large government order for shells for the famous dynamite guns used later, on the cruiser Vesuvius, in the Spanish-American War. This left an entire second floor of the factory unused.

Now ready to begin work, Charles hired his brother Frank with a raise of about 10 percent over the salary he got from Ames.

As Frank Duryea related to the Smithsonian Institution, he first removed the body of the buggy, with its springs, and placed it on a pair of wooden horses. There it

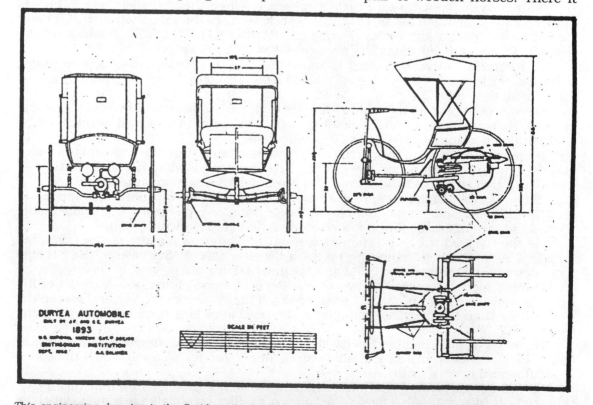

This engineering drawing in the Smithsonian Institution for the Duryea automobile is dated 1893 and indicates "built by F. & C.E. Duryea."

remained, until the summer of the following year. Then, the rear axle was removed and taken to a blacksmith's shop where the old axles were cut off and welded to a new drop-center axle. The front axle was removed, the ends of the axle slotted and webbed, C-shaped pieces carrying the kingpin bearings were fitted into each slot. These were braced from underneath by short brackets which were riveted and brazed in place.

The old spindles were welded to the center of the offset kingpins. These, which in turn, were mounted in their bearings in the same manner as the frame of the Columbia high-wheel bicycle was mounted in its fork. Arms welded to the lower end of the kingpin were connected by tie rods to an arm on the lower end of the vertical steering column on the center of the axle.

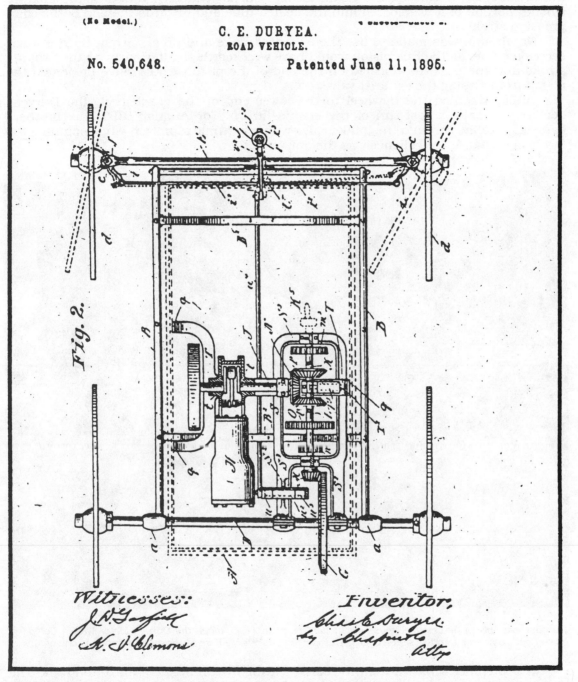

Charles E. Duryea's name appears on this blueprint for a road vehicle bearing a June 11, 1895 patent date. The plan of this vehicle varies from that of the original 1892-1893 Duryea.

Meanwhile, work began on the engine. Castings were poured for an engine which looked like a piece of cast iron pipe. It had no water jacket to cool itself. The Duryeas thought the open air would keep it cool. The head was cast as a thick disc, with both intake and exhaust valves located inside.

It was conceived by the inventor that "fired by the hot-tube ignition system, the force of the explosion would drive both pistons down, forcing the outer one tight against the head of the smaller one and, at the end of the stroke, the longer wall of the outer piston would strike an arm projecting into the cylinder near the open end, moving forward the exhaust valve rod to which the arm was attached, thus pushing open the valve in the head." At least this is what Duryea said in his letter of March 21, 1922, in which he related the car's history to C.W. Mitman.

On its exhaust stroke, the unrestrained outer piston moved all the way to the head, expelling all of the products of combustion and pushing the exhaust valve shut again. With a bore of four inches or less, Charles believed the engine would develop about three horsepower and run at a speed between 350-400 revolutions per minute.

Since no ignition system had yet been provided, they prepared a 4-1/2-inch length of one-quarter-inch iron pipe, closed at one end, and screwed the open end into the head. Heating this tube with an alcohol burner caused ignition of the mixture when a portion of it was forced into the heated tube and towards the end of the compression stroke.

No attempt was made to use the electrical make-and-break circuit used in their second engine, as the free piston would have wrecked the igniter parts on the exhaust stroke and the push-rod located on the end of the piston would have prevented the piston from closing the exhaust valve.

After attaching the flywheel to the lower end of the crankshaft, the Duryeas decided to make a test-run of the engine. In July or August 1892, the brothers sprayed gasoline through the intake valve with a perfume atomizer, while spinning the flywheel by hand. Dull silence was the only result.

The first example of automotive "mass production" came in 1896, when the Duryea Motor Wagon Company turned out 13 nearly identical automobiles. This car from the Henry Ford Museum's collection is one of them.

In September, Charles went to Peoria, leaving the unfinished "auto" to Frank. The carriage had no carburetor. After studying the format of a number of gasoline engines in a catalog, Frank Duryea developed his own carburetor.

Now Frank was ready for a test that he ran indoors. Duryea spun the flywheel with his big hands. Again and again in spun. No ignition.

Next, Duryea built a new and longer ignition tube. With this, he got a few "sputty" explosions, but nothing continuous. He went back to work. In February 1893, another test-run was started. A witness was present at this trial.

Will Russell, who left his testimonial at the Smithsonian on April 20, 1926, said, "Frank, standing to the right of the engine and behind the rear axle, reached forward and with the combination tiller-belt-shifter, moved the belt into drive position after the motor had been started.

"The carriage started forward, but as it approached the wall of the buildings, Frank discovered that he could not get the belt back into the neutral position. In desperation, he grasped the rear axle with both hands and was dragged a short distance, attempting to stop the machine before it struck the wall. Only slight damage resulted."

However ineffective, the machine ran. With every failure Frank learned to correct an ineffective part. The flywheel was too light; the pistons needed rings; there had to be a speed governor; the ignition was bad. So it went.

Winthrop Rockefeller owned two Duryeas, including this 1896 model. The design of this car was patterned after that of the Duryea that competed in the 1895 CHICAGO TIMES-HERALD race.

Frank blue-printed many improvements and gave them to a foundry and machinist. Then, he went off to get married. On August 28, 1893, Frank wrote to Charles that he would test-run the carriage outdoors on the coming Saturday, "off somewhere so no one will see us."

On September 21, the Duryea automobile was rolled onto an elevator. It was too long for the elevator, so they tipped the machine so that the entire weight (750-pounds) was on the rear wheels.

Once outside, they pushed it into an area between the Russell and Stonely buildings. After dark, a horse pulled the car out to a barn on Spruce Street, near Florence Street. Here the first runs were made".

Grabbing the flywheel Frank gave a mighty tug. Nothing happened. Again and again he tried. Then, feebly, the engine started with a roar and smoke. Frank jumped in and applied the clutch. The car moved! It drove 25-feet and stalled. Another start and it went 200-feet.

The results were not too encouraging. As Frank wrote Charles: "Have tried it finally and quit trying until some changes are made. Belt transmission very bad. Engine all right."

In October, Frank met Charles at the Columbian Exposition in Chicago and they discussed the machine and visited all the exhibits dealing with automotive progress. Frank was impressed with a Daimler quadricycle and its performance. They decided to give their auto one more chance with the old transmission.

On November 19, 1893, a test rider named Will Bemis was enlisted to ride the vehicle. (It had no brakes and failure of the transmission on a down-grade could be disastrous.) The *SPRINGFIELD MORNING UNION* gave a description of the run:

"Residents in the vicinity of Florence Street flocked to the windows yesterday afternoon astonished to see, gliding by in the roadway, a common top carriage with no shafts and no horse attached ...

"Mr. Bemis started from the corner of Hancock Avenue and Spruce Street and went up the avenue, up Hancock Street, and started down Florence Street, working finely, but when about halfway down the latter street, it stopped short, refusing to move. Investigation showed that the bearing had been worn smooth by the friction and a little water sprinkled upon it put it in running condition again."

The financier Erwin Markham, however, was not too impressed. He threatened to cut off support. Frank drew plans for a new geared transmission and managed to gain partial support. Money for material and use of the shop was to continue, but Frank was to complete the work on his own, without a salary.

Frank worked in a hurry for the next three months. He completely revised the transmission. When he was ready to make another test-run, he realized that it would have to be on icy, snow-covered roads. Would the iron tires have enough traction to move the carriage?

So, he devised an iron "snow tire." Jack Swaine, a local blacksmith made detachable rims studded with calks in two rows. On January 18, 1894 a test run was made. The next day he wrote Charles:

"Took out carriage again last night and gave it another test run about 9 o'clock." The only difficulty he mentioned was a slight irregularity in the engine caused by the tiny leather pad in the exhaust valve mechanism falling out. Relating, the incident to the Smithsonian Institution in 1956, Frank said "When I got this car ready to run one night, I took it out and I had a young fellow with me; I thought I might need him to help push in case the car didn't work. . . We ran from the area of the shop where it was built and ran up Washington Street hill. Then we drove along over level roads from there to the home of Mr. Markham where we refilled the water tank, which was boiling furiously, with water. We turned back and drove down along Central Street hill and along Maple, crossed into State Street, dropped down to Dwight and went west along Dwight, to the vicinity where we had a shed that we could put the car in for the night. We had run six miles."

Work was now begun on a new model with a host of improvements. When it was finished in 1895, it was entered in the Thanksgiving Day race sponsored by the *CHICAGO TIMES-HERALD*. The route was from Chicago to Evanston, Illinois and back.

Matched against two electric automobiles and three German Benz machines, Duryea won the race. This was achieved even though he accidentally took a two- mile detour. His 1,208-pound car, with its 57-1/2-inch wheelbase and wheels 55-inches high, roared 5.05 miles per hour for the 52-mile run.

In 1896, Frank made plans for a more powerful machine. That year their car won the Cosmopolitan race from New York City to Irvington-on-the-Hudson, New York.

During 1896, the Duryea Motor Wagon Company turned out 13 identical automobiles. This was the first example of mass production in American automobile history. The Smithsonian recognized this auto as the "first marketable automobile in America."

Another car that was part of the Winthrop Rockefeller Collection exhibited at the Museum of Automobiles was this 1903 Duryea Trap. This model was built in both Peoria, Illinois and Reading, Pennsylvania.

Frank took a machine to England and drove it himself on November 14, 1896 in the Liberty Day Run from London to Brighton. In this way he hoped to attract foreign capital. He later admitted this was a mistake and that he should have stayed at home to enlist American money. In 1898, both brothers sold their interest in the company and pursued separate careers.

In 1901, Frank Duryea joined the J. Stevens Arms and Tool Company, of Chicopee Falls, Massachusetts. There, automobiles were built under his supervision. In 1904, the Stevens-Duryea Company was formed with Frank as vice president and chief engineer.

During 10 years, the company produced a number of popular models. Among them was a 1907 light six known as the Model U and a large 1908 four-cylinder car called the Model X. A larger six, the Model Y, came in 1909. In 1914, Stevens retired and Frank took complete control, but in 1915 he sold out and also retired.

Charles Duryea relocated in Reading, Pennsylvania, where he produced autos under the name of the Duryea Power Company. Under this and other names, he built autos, vacuum cleaners, and other mechanical devices. However, he too soon faded from the automotive picture.

All in all, it was the Duryeas who had set the ball bearings rolling for the greatest industrial enterprise in the nation. Other auto factories mushroomed so fast that, seven years after their first race in 1895, factories were building 200 different makes of cars.

What happened to that first Duryea automobile? It was preserved. After the Duryea Motor Wagon Company was formed in 1895, company treasurer D.A. Reed put it in his barn. It remained there until 1920, when it was obtained by Inglis M. Uppereu and presented to the U.S. National Museum of the Smithsonian Institution. There, millions of Americans were able to view it annually. If ever a symbol of American ingenuity and free enterprise were needed, one had only to peruse the Duryea automobile.

The Duryea brothers built many different types of cars in several locations. This high-wheel model from the Imperial Palace Auto Collection is what is known as a Buggyaut model.

1896 Duryea Motor carriage. One of the first production run of 13 cars.

1900 Duryea dos-a-dos built by Charles Duryea in Reading, Pennsylvania.

1904 Stevens-Duryea. Frank Duryea joined the Massachusetts firm in 1901.

1904 Stevens-Duryea Model L Stanhope built by Stevens Arms & Tool Company.

1924 Stevens-Duryea. In 1906, Stevens-Duryea became an independent firm. Frank Duryea stayed until 1915, but left when a line of cheaper cars was built. Westinghouse then bought the firm. This Model G vestibule limousine dates from the last year of full production, though cars were built on order until 1927.

The Naming of the Automobile

By Richard J. Sagall

For the automobile to rise to its current position in the world, many problems had to be overcome. Mechanical functions presented the greatest obstacles. Then there were problems with public acceptance, legal problems and others. One problem hardly mentioned or remembered today caused as much concern around the turn of the century as any of these problems. It was what to call this new, sputtering and smelly device.

Probably the first term used was horseless carriage. This was an obvious and natural choice. It was descriptive of what these early vehicles looked like and also expressed the public viewpoint. The use of a modified term, rather than a new one, might be reflective of a sense that this device was a passing fancy rather than something to be taken seriously.

It is impossible to say when a common term was finally accepted. One landmark might be when the *NEW YORK TIMES* stopped refering to these machines as horseless carriages and began using the newer term automobile. This change took place in 1899. During the same year, there were many letters to the editor of the *NEW YORK TIMES* discussing this subject. Readers debated the pros and cons of various names and made suggestions of new ones.

The term automobile is of French origin. It was proposed by the French Academy to cover self-propelled vehicles that didn't run on tracks. An editorial in the *NEW YORK TIMES* of January 3, 1899 suggested the word was half Greek and half Latin and "so near indecent we print it with hesitation." However, the editorial went on to say "speakers of the English language have been fatally attracted by the irrelevant word horseless." The *TIMES* concluded, "It really looks as if the dispossessed or to-be-dispossessed animals (horses) are to get revenge on ungrateful humanity by stumping us to find a respectable name for our noisy and odorous machines."

Perhaps many readers of the *NEW YORK TIMES* took this last sentence as a challenge, for there was a lively correspondence proposing new names and criticizing those previously put forth. A brief survey of some of the terms suggested during this controversy illustrates both the interest in the problem, and perhaps some tongue-in-cheek humor. One reason for the interest might be reflected in the question, "How often do people have a role in determining a new word?"

One suggestion that appeared early in 1899 was autowein. It was claimed to be more euphonious than autotruck, a previously suggested word. But, both words, according to another editorial, "mean little of anything and nothing of what they intend to mean because there is something uncanny about these new-fangled vehicles. They are all unutterably ugly and never one of them has been provided with a good, or even endurable, name."

The July 3, 1899 issue of the *NEW YORK TIMES* contained a host of letters about this topic, each with its own suggestions. One letter confronts the problem of what to call the electric-automobile-horseless carriage. First, it is noted, "These could be referred to as oxen-less vehicles as readily as horse-less." Then, with much foresight, the writer stated, "Furthermore, the time is coming when the vehicle drawn by horses will be the one to excite remarks and the present novelty will be a thing of ordinary use." Not too bad a thought for 1899.

The writer then quickly dismissed the problem of what type of motive force is used by pointing out that it makes no difference to most people "so long as it runs safely, comfortably and quickly." This writer's final point, before his suggestions, is that we are a people that are busy and tend to shorten names. Examples, such as bike for bicycle and wire me instead of telegraph me were noted. His conclusion was that the best solution was to add a suffix to the already existing words. He proposed "-ine" as the ideal suffix. Thus, cab would become cabine, victoria changes to victorine, etc. His letter ended with, "Do I get the laurel?"

The same issue of the *TIMES* contained other suggestions for what to call the automobile, such as sineque (pronounced sineck and meaning without horse), selfmotors, mobiles (which could be shortened to "billys"), autogo, molectros and, finally, otto.

Later, in July, a writer to the *TIMES* was so moved by this problem he expressed his ideas in a poem. Although this suggestion might not be the best, he deserves note for his rhyme:

The struggles of each correspondent
In seeking proper nomenclature
Would make a verbophile despondent
And lose his faith in human nature
At least, that's how I feel
Away with Greek and Latin hybrids!
Auto's, Electro's and all such like
Contortions of title
By which word-coiners make their sly bids
For fame and glory.
(These I'd much like
For my own requital: But why?)
I have the proper
Name for these horseless apparati
It's simply Goalone.
That's Anglo-Saxon, I will bet a copper,
And it's original: to that I
Make my proud boast to own.

Though the *NEW YORK TIMES* carried this lively discussion, other publications had a hand in what was going on. In September 1899, in the first issue of *THE AUTO-MOBILE* magazine, an editorial defended the use of the term automobile against the objections that it was of French origin. It pointed out the word was intelligible in English. The editorial then proposed the word automobilism to cover any phase of motoring. Finally, they deemed the use of "mobe," as a shortened version of automobile, totally unacceptable.

Perhaps the first publication to get into this problem was the *CHICAGO TIMES-HERALD*. In 1895, the newspaper sponsored its famous race. As a part of the event the editor, H.H. Kohsaat, also had a contest to come up with a name for the horseless carriage. The first prize of $500, went to motocycle. Quadracycle took second. Petrocar was third.

The *SCIENTIFIC AMERICAN* of July 22, 1899 also presented a list of names. The writer expressed a preference for autopher. He claimed it was derived from St. Christopher's name. He expressed a dislike for kinetic, autokinet and outokin, stating that he found them "particularly atrocious."

In 1899, the *ELECTRICAL REVIEW* ran a contest for the best name to apply to "electrically propelled, self-contained vehicles for roads and streets." First prize of $10 went to electromobile. The second prize of $5 was awarded for the same name. The *NEW YORK TIMES* of June 12, 1899 commented on the name: "The *ELECTRICAL REVIEW* safely might offer millions to anyone who would make a worse name."

In 1901, *LIFE* magazine liked the word automobility. This refered to the "class of people caught up in the new craze."

To add a foreign note to this topic, Greek papers around the turn of the century referred to motor vehicles as automaxa. Prince Borghese, during the Peking-to-Paris race in 1907, found that the Chinese referred to autos as "chi-cho." This means "fire chariot." In England, the common term motor-car is said to have been coined by F.R. Simms, founder of the British Daimler Company.

Considering that early cars like this 1887 Copeland looked quite unusual, it's not difficult to understand why finding a name for them was a challenge taken up by many period publications.

1901 Gasmobile. This could have become a generic term for gas-powered cars, with steamers becoming stea-mobiles and electrics becoming electromobiles.

1901 Autocar Type VI standard runabout. If Autocar hadn't been used as a trade name, it could have been adopted as a general term for the automobile.

1902 Automotor. This is another car with a name that could have become a generic term for the motor vehicle.

The Odyssey of the Thomas Flyer

By Phil Cole

In February 1908, the *NEW YORK TIMES* and *LE MATIN* sponsored the first Great Race. This was a 22,000-mile jaunt (13,000 miles over land) from Times Square to the Champs Elysee. Entered at the last moment, a Flyer automobile made by the Thomas Motor Car Company of Buffalo, N.Y. was the sole United States entry.

On February 11, George Schuster, a trouble-shooter for Thomas, took a car to a potential buyer in Providence, Rhode Island. The prospect was unhappy with his Pope-Hartford. He'd heard that Thomas required every car built to climb hills, in high gear, at 55-60 miles per hour before it was delivered.

Returning to the Thomas distributor in Providence, Schuster found a phone call waiting. The next day, a rather stunned trouble-shooter left New York City as the mechanic on a 1907 Thomas Flyer heading west-bound in a race around the world.

This occurred at a time when newspaper competition was vicious. Publications underwrote and created news to out do their competitors. The goal was increased circulation. Races, such as the *CHICAGO TIMES-HERALD* contest of 1895, became a marketing tool for the fledgling auto business. So it came as little surprise that a race preceding the around-the-world race was sponsored by *LE MATIN*, a leading French publication.

It was done by *LE MATIN* to spotlight the supposed superiority of French automobiles, but none of the cars from that nation ran in the money. An Italian car won and a German car came in second, but circulation still jumped. Soon, the concept of a "Great Race" that would circle the globe was dreamed up to prove the previous contest a fluke.

This was planned to be the longest auto race ever held. It was and, in fact, it still is. Three cars from France, one from Germany and one from Italy were entered. All five showed up in New York. A sixth vehicle, the Thomas Flyer, entered the day before the start. The *NEW YORK TIMES* had linked itself with *LE MATIN* as a co-sponsor. French reporters covered French cars. The *NEW YORK TIMES* sent a reporter and a photographer along on the Flyer.

The race was planned to start on Abraham Lincoln's birthday. Times Square was crammed with 250,000 people on that February 12 in 1908. Some cars lined up abreast. The Thomas Flyer, as official host vehicle, was parked at the curb.

E.R. Thomas said his entry was "stock," a situation that his mechanics altered when the cars reached Buffalo two days later. Montague Roberts was the driver. Two other men relieved him later. George Schuster was driver-designate for the fun part of the event overseas.

This photograph was taken on July 30, 1908 when thousands of New Yorkers welcomed home the victorious Thomas Flyer.

New York City Mayor George B. McClelland was to fire a pistol to start the race. He was nowhere to be seen. Later he explained that he couldn't get through the crowd. Promoters went to a second plan and AAA official Colgate Hoyt fired the "shot heard 'round Times Square." The Great Race was underway and the field roared up Broadway.

The route went across the northern United States so the cars could run on frozen roads, rivers and cow paths. Three weeks later, after hitting bogs, mires, swamps, floods and railroad ties, the intrepid travelers limped into San Francisco. So torturous was the going that the *TIMES* reported it exactly as it happened. No hyperbole was necessary to increase reader interest. The truth was stranger than fiction.

This original photograph shows the Thomas car fording a stream in Siberia as the 1908 around-the-world race went through Russia.

The so-called race committee changed the rules often. While some cars were en route to Seattle and Alaska by ship, a decision was made to reroute others. They were to go to Japan, cross that less than 100-mile wide island, and then be shipped to Asia where the final overland portion was to begin. Someone forgot to tell all the entrants. For a while, the contestants didn't know where to go. The officials didn't realize that Japan had no roads. There were only paths over its steep geography. The right-angle turns required coolies to lift each car and physically carry it around the corners.

The entire trip through Asia and Europe was filled with problems. There was a bizarre quality to the finish. French gendarmes were miffed since their cars had again run behind the Germans and Italians, not to mention the American entry. So, they insisted that the Flyer have headlamps burning when it entered Paris at twilight.

George Schuster asked and got permission to take a bicycle lamp from a child. He discovered the lamp wouldn't come off the bicycle. While French police fumed, Schuster and crew put the boy and bike, with its lamp burning, in front of the dashboard and chugged down Champs Elysee to the finish.

The Flyer was actually the second vehicle to cross the finish line. The German car, driven by Lieutenant Hans Koeppen, was first. However, penalties for route changes and rules violations cost Koeppen a total of 26 days. When the final results were tabulated, the Flyer won by nearly a month.

Once the judges determined that the Thomas was the winner, a triumphant return to the United States followed. Schuster turned down invitations of honorariums in England. He was given a hero's welcome back in New York.

In Buffalo, a mile-long parade, a dinner with 1,000 white-tied and tailed guests, and huzzahs from the mayor and the president of the Automobile Club of America showed the city's appreciation. Eventually, though, the jubilation faded. Schuster went back to work, the *TIMES* switched circulation promotions, and the Flyer was retired to an experimental laboratory at the Thomas factory.

George Schuster was denied a bonus. He couldn't collect on deals offered him. Thomas Motor Car Company had no better luck. Later cars, attempting to be successors to the Great Race winner, turned out failures. Schuster lobbied for Thomas to build better quality products to protect both his and the race car's reputation. He became provoked at the lackluster planning, poor engineering and slipshod assembly work he was seeing. Finally, he left Thomas and moved to Boston to work as the service manager for an automobile dealer.

On Abraham Lincoln's birthday, in 1908, the race began at Times Square, in New York City. A crowd estimated at 250,000 people turned out to see the cars off.

The Flyer parked near Fournier's Garage, in Paris, France, at the end of the 1908 race. The driver and his crew look happy, but weary.

This is the Thomas Flyer "Pathfinder" parked in New York City. It was part of a 1909 sales promotion a year after winning the event that is known as the New York-to-Paris Race or simply the "Great Race."

This is how the 1907 Thomas Flyer looked after years of storage and abuse. The late Henry Austin Clark, Jr. rescued the historic vehicle and preserved it for many years at his Long Island Automotive Museum.

By mid-1912, only four years after it had been in the spotlight of the automotive world, the Thomas company went into receivership. A sale was held to liquidate the firm's assets. Charles E. Finnegan, of Elma, New York bought lot no. 1 in the bankruptcy sale. It included the Thomas Flyer that had been used on the Great Race, a couple of fire engines, six other cars, a bus and repair parts, all for $51,000.

Finnegan disposed of everything but the rusting Thomas that had won the race. He stored it in his garage for 33 years. Parts were missing, the tires were gone and rust and decay had taken a toll. Yet, the famous car was preserved.

After World War II, Americans developed a yen for old cars. Opera singer James Melton was a famous early collector. He learned that the Flyer still existed and expressed an interest in obtaining it. Melton contacted George Schuster, who then made a trip to Elma to verify the originality of the car.

Schuster was indecisive about the cars's authenticity. He was unable to find some angle iron and boiler plate with which on-the-road repairs had been done during the race. Melton backed off on purchasing the vehicle, but Frances V. DuPont of Wilmington, Delaware, bought it for her husband. It eventually went to her estate, where it sat untouched for three years. Then, it was sold to Henry Austin Clark Jr. for his Long Island Auto Museum. Clark exhibited the car it untouched condition until 1963, when *READERS DIGEST* did an interview with Schuster about the race. By then, he was the only surviving competitor.

The article fanned considerable interest in Reno, Nevada, where casino owner Bill Harrah had taken an interest in antique cars. Harrah bought what was left of the car from "Austie." Clark even threw in the Great Race trophy, which was a silver base surmounted by a globe. To verify the authenticity of the car, Schuster came to Reno to check it once more. This time, some holes that had been drilled in the chassis for race repairs were discovered. He then confirmed it was the champ.

Harrah's craftsman George Herman supervised a restoration of the famous Thomas Flyer. Craftsman returned the car to its condition at the end of the race. On June 11, 1964, Schuster took the wheel and waved to onlookers as he drove the Flyer from suburban Sparks, Nevada to Harrah's Casino in downtown Reno. It was later given a place of honor at Harrah's Auto Collection.

(Editor's note: Article and photos courtesy of GreatRace Limited, organizers of the modern Interstate Batteries Great American Race).

This is how the 1907 Thomas that won the New York-to-Paris Race of 1908 looked after it was restored by Harrah's Auto Collection. The Model 35 had a 70-horsepower four-cylinder engine and sold for $4,500.

This is a rear view showing how the car looked after restoration in Bill Harrah's shops. Note the authentic touches like the suitcase, ropes and American flag.

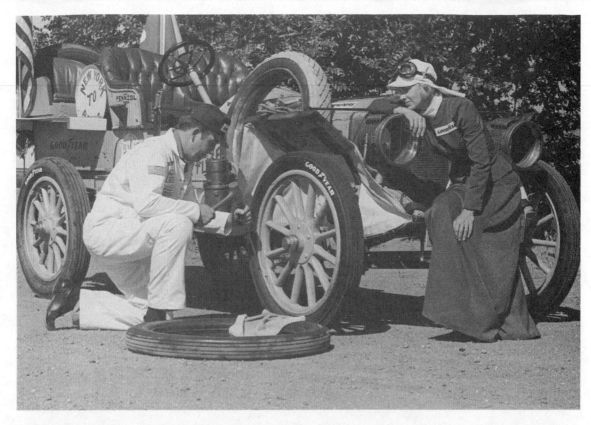

In 1986, Newt and Ginni Withers drove the 1907 Thomas Flyer from Disneyland, in California, to New York City in the modern Great American Race. Here we see Withers changing one of the Goodyear tires on the historic car.

The car in action during the 1986 Great American Race. The Withers donated $25,000 to the William F. Harrah Foundation in exchange for the use of the Flyer as a Goodyear-sponsored entrant in the GAR.

100 Years of Autos Showcased in Henry Ford Museum

By John A. Gunnell

The automobile has had a tremendous impact on Americans and their nation. Since its creation, nearly 100 years ago, this wonderful machine has affected every aspect of life in the United States. Each year of the 20th century has felt its impact. The way we work, the way we play and the way we relax have all been changed by the horseless carriage.

Until 1987, the average person had virtually no way to really experience the reshaping of our society during the automotive age. Books, films and museums existed that all did a fine job of highlighting automotive history. Yet, there were very few efforts to look at the car in a broader context, viewing it as an instrument of cultural change.

Henry Ford Museum's "The Automobile in American Life" exhibition corrected this deficiency. Opening in November 1987, it was a major attempt to study the weaving of automotive history into the tapestry of everyday life. Covering a physical area totaling four acres, it represented an investment of $6 million in a complete remodeling of nearly half of the museum.

"Our intention is to make the automotive story more interesting and appealing to our vistors," museum president Harold K. Skramstad noted on October 14, 1986, upon announcing plans to build the exhibit. He explained that numerous additions, including full-sized buildings, would significantly enlarge "a collection that is already one of the most comprehensive in the world."

The full-sized buildings included a 1940s style filling station, a restored 1946 diner and a replica of a Holiday Inn motel room from the 1960s. Other automotive-related elements to be included were a drive-in movie theater, a replica of a highway ramp and a neon sign from a McDonald's fast-food restaurant.

Albert H. Woods and Associates was hired to direct the master plan and design of the exhibition. An honorary advisory committee comprised of top executives from domestic and foreign automobile companies was announced and auto historian George S. May was appointed to serve as a consultant. The master plan was to organize the exhibition around six different themes that tied the automobile and its life-style influences together.

The Evolving American Car

The first part of the exhibit was called "Evolution of the American Automobile and its Industry." It featured a variety of cars parked on a raised highway, beginning with the latest models and tracing backwards through eight phases of history:

1965-1986: Emergence of a Global Industry
1945-1965: The Boom Years
1929-1945: Facing New Challenges
1920-1929: The "Big Three" Appear
1908-1920: The Industry Grows Up
1896-1908: The Birth of an Industry
1769-1896: Origins of the American Automobile

Artist's sketch shows the basic design of Henry Ford Museum's "The Automobile in American Life" exhibition.

To represent the earliest phase, such vehicles as an 1865 horse-drawn Flint phaeton; an 1891 Sylph Duryea bicycle; an 1865 Roper steam carriage, an 1885 Benz model; and an 1896 Duryea Motor Wagon were featured. The second phase included an 1899 Locomobile; a 1900 Winton; a 1901 Baker electric; a 1903 Olds, Ford and Cadillac; and a 1904 Rambler. Later highlights were a 1923 Copper-cooled Chevrolet; 1924 Chrysler; 1940 Oldsmobile show chassis with Hydra-Matic Drive; a 1948 Tucker; a 1950 Rambler; a 1960 Corvair; and the first Honda built in America.

In all, the section featured 40 complete vehicles, two show chassis and a pair of auto bodies, supplemented by several video presentations and extensive displays of literature, photos and motoring accessories. Walking alongside the serpentine highway was somewhat like walking into the pages of this book, except that you were able to see the cars and artifacts face-to-face. The cars covered 100 years of automotive history and gave a firsthand look at how the automobile progressed from a custom creation to a mass-production item.

Advertising the American Car

Methods of advertising and promoting automobiles, from public exposures of concept cars to wheel-to-wheel auto racing were also examined by the exhibition. This section of The Automobile in American Life used cars, memorabilia, advertisements and billboards to carry its theme across.

Among the automotive highlights featured were Ford's "999" race car from 1902; a famous 1903 Packard named "Old Pacific" that made a cross-country endurance run; a 1909 Sears; a 1914 Detroit Electric; the 1951 Buick LeSabre prototype; and a 1964 Ford Mustang. Auto stunt driving shows, early advertising slogans (See page 106); and sales jingles from the 1950s were all covered.

Holiday Inn sign from the 1960s was part of the exhibition's "Automotive Landscape" section.

American Symbol

Section three of the showcase was called "The Automobile as an American Symbol." This was an attempt to explore the image of certain vehicles and the fact that car buyers are often motivated by a Walter Mitty complex that steers them towards the image that a specific model projects. The actual cars featured included a 1923 Stutz Bearcat; a 1926 Rolls-Royce; a 1927 Ford Model T; a 1930 Bugatti Royale; a 1949 Mercury coupe styled by Barris Kustoms; and a 1965 Pontiac GTO.

General Motors loaned the 1951 Buick LeSabre (top) and the 1939 Buick Y-Job (bottom) concept vehicles to the Henry Ford Museum.

These cars were selected to illustrate various symbolic meanings that Americans have attached to the automobile in using the car as an expression of their ambitions, desires and dreams.

American Style

Both production cars and cars-of-the-future played a major role in the exhibition's next section called "Designing the Automobile." In addition, scale models; sketches and renderings; videos; audio tapes; and other display aids were used to focus attention on advances in automobile designing.

The museum was able to borrow the famous 1939 Buick Y-Job from General Motors to be the crown jewel of this section. Other automobile highlights included a 1927 LaSalle; a 1937 Cord; the 1953 Ford X-100; the 1958 Firebird III; and a 1963 Studebaker Avanti.

Design-work from the 1920s, 1930s, 1940s and 1950s reflected the various developments in design trends, as well as the different tools and techniques used by auto stylists over the past 70 years.

Neon signs from Laney's Diner and vintage McDonald's seem to go well with the styling of a 1956 Lincoln and 1959 Cadillac.

Getaway Vehicles

"Getting Away From it All" was the name of section five of The Automobile in American Life. It included a pair of early camp trucks (1915 Packard and 1921 White); a 1929 Packard roadster; a 1947 MG-TC; a 1951 Crosley Hot Shot; and a 1959 Volkswagen Camper. The theme focused on the freedom that the automobile gave to Americans; the ability to go where they wanted, when they wanted.

This installation centered around an actual wooded campsite where the camping vehicles were displayed complete with authentic outdoor gear from the appropriate eras. Also featured was a rich collection of diaries, books, magazines, postcards, snapshots, and vacation brochures. The other sporty vehicles seen were selected on the basis of their leisure driving appeal and their purely-for-fun characteristics.

Land Ho, Ho!

The last section of the exhibition, and probably the most fun to see, was called "The Automotive Landscape." It showcased an especially bright and colorful display of a number of interesting vehicles placed against the backdrop of vintage architecture.

"Delivering" fuel to a 1940s Texaco gas station (discovered in Kingston, Massachusetts) was a 1939 Dodge Airflow gas truck painted a very bright red. Parked below the McDonald's "golden arches" was a blue-and-white 1956 Chevrolet ragtop. A 1911 Saxon; a 1929 Ford Model A; a 1937 Chrysler Airflow; and a 1956 Ford Thunderbird were also seen. Visitors were able to sit inside a big-band era diner (moved from Hudson, Massachusetts); to see an early miniature golf course; to peek inside the Holiday Inn; or to time-travel back to 1941 to inspect a tourist cabin from Michigan's rustic Irish Hills region.

Interspersed with the large-scale artifacts were a variety of signs, photos, graphics, films and other automobilia. It was all part of an attempt to convey how cars helped create a new mobile lifestyle and how they influenced structures erected alongside the growing network of coast-to-coast highways.

Installation of The Automobile in American Life exhibition was a major step for any institution, even one as large as Henry Ford Museum and Greenfield Village. Prior to the time that work commenced in 1986, the automobile collection there had been largely unchanged for over 50 years.

To create a proper reflection of interpretive history, extensive discussions were held with historians and specialists in pop culture. This brought about the decision to divide the exhibition into six sections.

In addition to improvements in the physical plant, the work entailed listing objects needed for the display. Next came the task of determining whether each item was "stored in the attic" or whether it had to be obtained from outside. Included on the list were over 100 antique autos; the gas station; the diner; the tourist cabin; bicycles; motorcycles; neon signs; horse-drawn vehicles; billboards; films; recordings; ads; photos; artwork; menus; maps; and even diaries.

Drawings of the exhibition's design were produced and a scale-model was built. This meant getting the exact specifications of each vehicle down to 1/8-inch scale. Lighting, the placement of video monitors, sight-lines, and the installation of various props were other considerations. Then, mechanical drawings of the exhibit were done and developed into blueprints for each structural component.

Under the supervision of exhibits manager Tom Elliott and his chief assistant Dave Scott, hands-on work began in November 1986. Almost 100 museum employees and 42 sub-contractors toiled to get the exhibition ready on schedule. The door opened to the public right on time on November 7, 1987.

Symbolically, this early touring car is heading in the "opposite direction" from the 1950 Rambler and Buick on the upper ramp.

Editor's note: The "Automobile in American Life" is still on view at the Henry Ford Museum & Greenfield Village, 20900 Oakwood Boulevard, Dearborn, MI 48121-1970. Anyone interested in information about the exhibition can call (313) 271-1620. On June 16-23, 1996 the Antique Automobile Club of America (AACA) is scheduled to hold an official "Centennial of the American Automobile Industry" meet in Dearborn, Michigan. Henry Ford Museum & Greenfield Village will host the meet's judging event. Ralph Boyer, a well-known Detroit AACA activist who attended the auto industry's 1946 "Golden Jubilee" celebration as a boy, will be chairman of the Centennial of the American Automobile Industry meet. Automotive historian Randy Mason will be assistant chairman. Details about the meet can be obtained from AACA, 501 West Governor Road, Hershey, PA 17033.

Customized Mercury restyled by George Barris (top) is one of more than 100 cars in the exhibition. Serpentine highway (bottom) holds 40 vehicles.

When completed in 1987, the exhibition represented the first major change in the Henry Ford Museum's auto display in over 50 years.

Visitors view models done by famous automotive designers in section of design exhibit that examines the styling process.

Remember when hamburgers cost only 15 cents and you could buy a Chevrolet convertible with options for under $3,000?

Model of Selden patent vehicle carries the date 1877, although it wasn't built until 1905 when Selden took Henry Ford to court.

Another of the many rare factory concept vehicles on display is the 1958 General Motors Firebird gas turbine car.

Two famous race cars in the show include Henry Ford's "999" (nearest camera) and the "Old Pacific" Packard runabout. Bicycles are included, too.

"Evolution of the Automobile and its Industry" takes viewer from Buicks built in Flint, Michigan to Hondas built in Marysville, Ohio.

First Mustang is featured in "Advertising and Promoting the Auto" section of exhibition, which explores the pony car's successful ad campaign.

Oldsmobile introduced Hydra-Matic Drive to the car show-going public with this special show chassis dating from 1940.

One of just a handful left from a fleet of Dodge Airflow tankers, this streamlined truck is parked in a 1940s vintage gas station.

"Designing the American Automobile" section of the exhibition features several notable styling milestones, including this Studebaker Avanti.

Celebrating 100 Years of American Cars

By Bob Stubenrauch

Welcome to the century of the American automobile. This is a year to celebrate those pioneers whose efforts have given us the modern automobile.

As children, most of us peered through the eyepiece of a kaleidoscope, that fascinating gadget of mirrors and colored bits of glass. We turned the tube until some dazzling design made us stop and gaze in awe. To celebrate the century of the American automobile, we will provide you with an imaginary kaleidoscope. You will see, recalled from the mist of time, the milestones of American automobile achievements that have brought us to where we are today, the most mobile people on earth.

The Beginnings

Historians and the industry agree that, among scores of pioneers, Gottlieb Daimler and Karl Benz began the age of the auto in Germany during 1885. These two succeeded where scores of predecessors had failed because they employed the new internal combustion gas engine as a power source.

Eight years after Benz drove his tricycle down the roads of Germany, the Duryea brothers of Springfield, Massachusetts were cruising about in their one-cylinder horseless carriage. It incorporated electric ignition and a spray carburetor, both designed and built by Frank Duryea.

By 1896, there was an American auto industry and several hundred horseless carriages were operating. In the next five years, dozens of auto factories opened, racing began and a livery stable in Boston converted to the "sales, storage and repair of motor vehicles." It was, in effect, the first service garage.

In rapid succession, Timken patented his tapered roller bearing, the first independent car dealer opened, the first auto insurance policy was issued and what would be the world's largest tire and rubber company opened for business in 1898 in Akron, Ohio. The *HORSELESS AGE* and the *MOTOR AGE* began publication, the first car buff periodicals.

James Ward Packard told the maker that he didn't think much of his newly purchased Winton automobile and formed a company to build a better motor car. Now the once remote prospect of a new age of transportation became a certainty. Not everyone welcomed the automobile though.

In America, each town made its own rules governing the motor car. One local auto ordinance required a motorist approaching a turn in the road to stop 100 yards away, toot his horn, ring a bell, fire a revolver and send up three bombs at five minute intervals before proceeding. In another town, should a horse balk and refuse to pass an oncoming auto, the motorist "must take the car apart as quickly as possible and conceal the parts in the grass." In 1902, the American Automobile Association was founded to dispel the widespread prejudice against the auto.

The newly perfected gas engine helped launch this explosive growth in the auto industry, but it would be another decade before the electric car and the steamer would finally give up the contest for power supremacy. However, hard tires of solid rubber gave way quickly to pneumatics and the industry owed thanks to a devoted father for that essential improvement. John Boyd Dunlop perfected a workable pneumatic tire in 1888. His motivation had been to provide a more comfortable ride for his invalid son's solid-tired wheelchair.

Mass-production arrived in 1901 when Oldsmobile built 500 cars of one model. An even more significant event that year was a gusher that came in at Spindletop, Texas. Crude oil dropped below five-cents a barrel.

In 1903 Autocar was the first multi-cylinder American car to have shaft-drive instead of the usual chain-drive. Its twin-cylinder design produced 3-1/2 horsepower. Autocar ceased making cars in 1911 but continued as a truck builder until becoming part of White Motor in recent years.

Production of autos skyrocketed. It soon became apparent in America that cars would be available to every level of society. In Europe, the bicycle would still be the workers' transportation long after domestic automakers had put a car within reach of the average American wage earner. During 1903, both a Winton and a Packard completed coast-to-coast runs across the primitive roads and trackless reaches of America. A single-cylinder model Packard made that crossing in 53 days, driven by Tom Fetch.

A 1911 Model T Ford owned by Andy Thorn of Akron, heads a line of antique autos that participated in the Goodyear event. Behind the T is Bill Haines Jr.'s 1914 Pierce.

Car Making Rockets Ahead

A dizzying period in our history began. Over 3,000 automakers would be launched in the U.S. market. Hundreds would never get beyond building a single prototype. Out of this incredible competition came continuous improvement. Cars became safer, faster, more dependable, easier to drive and simpler to service. In 1908, Cadillac won the coveted Dewar Trophy in England for the standardization test. Three cars were disassembled into a common pile of parts. Then three smooth-running cars were reassembled from the jumble. Even Rolls-Royce couldn't match that.

No celebration of automotive history would be complete without a Stanley Steamer. This one is a 1911 model owned by Otto Maier of Massillon, Ohio.

Cars grew sportier and racier. The 1910 American Underslung was so called because its frame was carried below the axles. Generating 70 horsepower from six cylinders, it was a powerhouse in its day.

Steam and electric autos were still popular with many motorists, despite the special problems each type had. Cars like the 1911 Stanley touring model had unbelievable acceleration. Frank Marriott proved this by posting a record 127 miles per hour in 1906. It was a speed mark that stood until the 1930s.

When the European War erupted in 1914, Ford had been building Model Ts for six years and had just introduced the moving assembly line. It was a car that helped put America on wheels. Its four-cylinder engine with planetary drive delivered 30 miles per gallon at a top speed of 45 miles per hour. In 1915, Henry Ford introduced another innovation called the rebate. He mailed each of 300,000 customers a $50 check when he surpassed his production goal.

Significant "firsts" were happening every month in those tumultuous years through 1920. Every conceivable type of engine was offered: The four, the six, the V-8, the 12. Hydraulic brakes had arrived, along with car heaters, a few all-steel bodies, the electric self-starter, electric lights and even an attempt at an automatic transmission. The elegant Pierce-Arrow had both a self-starter and electric lights and cost up to $6,000 ... the price of a dozen lesser runabouts.

A large crowd turned out to see the review of old cars and trucks representing 100 years of motor vehicle development.

Trucking Breaks Out of the City Limits

In 1918, Goodyear Tire & Rubber Company sent its fleet of Wingfoot Express trucks coast-to-coast in record time on huge pneumatic tires. This helped usher in a new transportation industry. Goodyear's restored 1917 Packard Wingfoot Express has been making cross-country promotions since 1984, visiting such events as the Great American Race and the Iola Old Car Show. While the next decade would see a growing shift to pneumatic tires on trucks, many commercials continued to ride on solid tires.

The Lincoln Highway Association was instrumental in improving roads and Henry Ford stunned the industry with his offer of $5-a-day to workers "of good character." Five million American cars were now registered. A future major automaker was born when Chevrolet joined General Motors in 1918. That same year saw a sharp decline in the sale of electrics such as the Rauch and Lang, the Detroit Electric and the Woods Dual-Power. Their low speed and limited range spelled their finish, despite the appeal of odor-free and silent operation.

The Roaring Twenties

The Roaring Twenties began with a whimper. A postwar recession dealt a body blow to new car sales and also produced the first-ever U.S. gasoline shortage. Despite the economic problems, the Indy 500 again drew large crowds and for the first time was broadcast on radio. The 1922 event-winning car was a Duesenberg. The same racing model had previously gone to Europe where it became the first American auto to win an international Grand Prix.

Sophistication of the auto rolled along, with more of the modern amenities becoming standard equipment. These included power windshield wipers, four-wheel brakes, engine air cleaners, balloon tires, gas gauges on the dash and even the luxury of an on-board radio. By now the federal government was funding some highway construction, while state highway departments were expanding the use of truck plows to keep the nation's new roads open through the winter months.

In 1923 the Model T was beginning to look dated, but Ford's policy of constantly lowering prices in response to increasing sales was still working. The runabout Model T was a steal at $265 that year.

By 1924, closed cars finally edged out tourings in popularity and the big news at the 24th National Automobile Show was the new Chrysler. It was the first car with a compression ratio as high as 4.5:1. (They would go up even more later, before heading back down again.) Only a few electrics and steamers, such as the Detroit Electric and the Doble steam car, still survived. This year, General Motors built a new "proving grounds" in Detroit and Goodyear opened a San Angelo, Texas tire testing facility.

There was a trend to straight-eight engines, a design that Packard and Buick would stay with into the 1950s. Cars like the eight-cylinder Packard Sport Phaeton featured bold color schemes thanks to new synthetic lacquers. New names arrived in the last half of the 1920s. Only a few were destined for long production runs. DeSoto, LaSalle, Plymouth, Ajax, Diana, Marquette, Viking and Pontiac were among the new marques.

William Reynolds, of Findlay, Ohio, exhibited his 1929 Model A Ford in front of the ultra-modern Goodyear Technical Center.

It was a time of contrasts. Kissel produced dashing Gold Bug Speedsters, while other companies built more modest family cars such as the 1928 Oldsmobile sedan. Ford finally closed out the Model T's production, at 15 million units, in May of 1927. This was a one-model record that would stand until the Volkswagen Beetle came along. The 1928 Model A Ford succeeded the T.

The Depression Decade

The American auto industry broke all the old records in 1929 with an output of 5,337,000 vehicles. Unfortunately, that record is not what we remember about 1929. Black Friday, the day the market crashed, will always be synonymous with recollections of that tragic year.

In one of Detroit's great ironies, the magnificent cars of the "Classic Age" arrived on the showroom floors as their potential customers were being wiped out in the market crash. The Marmon V-16, the Packard V-12 Speedster, the supercharged Duesenberg and the Cadillac V-16 were launched in a virtual sales vacuum. Marmon and Duesenberg would not survive the loss of their affluent customers.

So closed this decade of booming growth. The depression would have a sobering effect on Detroit. However, the auto industry would ride it out. Americans would survive the depression in Detroit, as they did on the farm and in the small town, with tenacity and ingenuity. Chrysler began selling cars in a wide price range. The custom-bodied Imperial dual cowl Phaeton was seen at the most exclusive country clubs, but it was the low-priced Plymouth that kept Chrysler afloat.

In 1932, General Motors' Oakland became the Pontiac, which hasn't slowed down since. The Pontiac was a medium-priced car selling for a price just pennies-per-day higher than cheap cars. It cost just under a thousand dollars. An 85-horsepower V-8 and synchromesh transmission were standard on the Series 302.

Despite the depression, a steady march of automotive improvements continued. In fact, heightened competition demanded each maker offer something new the others didn't have. Ford had put safety plate glass in the new Model A and soon it would become an industry standard. In 1931, car warranties were introduced. The "guarantee" was usually for 90 days or 4,000 miles, whichever came first. In that same year, total U.S. auto production since the turn of the century passed the 50 million mark.

The expression, "It's a Duesy" still means "it's the greatest." The Duesenberg Model J was. Fewer than 500 were built between 1928 and 1935. Chassis costs alone were $8,500 and a custom body doubled that figure. Could it go? Race driver Ab Jenkins made a 24-hour endurance run in 1935. He averaged 135.5 miles per hour in a supercharged Duesy that produced nearly 400 horsepower. This record stood until 1990, when it was broken by a Corvette. There are legends and the Duesenberg SJ is one of them. Its eight-cylinder engine displaced 420 cubic-inches and delivered 320 horsepower. The original cost in depression dollars was $17,750.

The Auto Changes Our Society

In 1933 an American institution was born with the opening of the first drive-in movie theater. President Franklin D. Roosevelt's "New Deal" was in full swing. As an employer of last resort, the U.S. Government launched vast public works projects, building everything from post offices and fire houses to airports, bridges and highways. The industry and the motorist were among the beneficiaries of these programs.

Much has been written on the impact of car ownership on society. This can be heavy going, so we'll recount just one incident that speaks volumes. Some of us lived through the Great Depression and all of us have seen the grim photographs and movies of America's struggle in the 1930s. At one point, even nature seemed to conspire against us, as wind and drought combined to create the "dust bowl." Thousands of farm families, unable to wrest a living from their now worthless land, piled their belongings in the old family car and headed for California.

Their suffering of the farmers was seen by all America in newsreels at the local movie house. Members of the Soviet ligation in Washington, D.C. saw this as an opportunity to denigrate America. They quickly bought up prints of these newsreels and released them in Russia, adding a sound track that described, all too accurately, the suffering of our farmers. Russians leaving the theaters were heard, however, to

Streamlining was a hot styling trend of the 1930s. This 1938 Lincoln-Zephyr owned by Vince Dornan of Attica, Ohio is a famous example.

remark, "America is an astonishing place because the farmers are the poorest people there, and yet they all have cars." The films were quickly withdrawn by the authorities.

The Stylist and Designer Arrive in Detroit

The conservative shape and upright lines of the family car hadn't changed much in a decade, but in the mid-1930s, bold new designers ushered in something called "streamlining." The Chrysler Airflow, the Cord 810/812, and the Lincoln Zephyr were strikingly different from anything that had gone before. The Airflow represented an engineering success, but a failure in the marketplace. The Cord was termed "the most beautiful car ever built" and was the first car the Museum of Modern Art would recognize as "rolling sculpture." A bit more successful with the buying public was the Lincoln Zephyr with its V-12 engine. These exotic cars were all upscale models. However, the median wholesale price of all Detroit's products had slumped to under $750. This reflected the austerity of the marketplace.

In 1938, the gear shift lever moved from the floor to the steering column, where it remains most commonly today, as the selector for an automatic transmission. Detroit became excited about a Goodyear innovation, the first Rayon passenger car tire, in 1938. That same year finally saw a perfected automatic gear change system. It was the predecessor of General Motors' Hydra-Matic Drive.

Everyone from Sturtevant to Reo had made earlier tries to develop an automatic transmission, but none proved really workable. Now every other maker was put on notice that this feature must be duplicated. Chrysler stayed with a low-cost, reliable semi-automatic until 1953. Packard made a complex unit called Ultramatic that nearly drove the company broke.

While auto sales slumped badly in 1938, a creeping tide of European orders for war goods helped Detroit. The New York World's Fair in 1939 gave the industry a chance to dazzle the public. Pontiac did it by displaying a transparent 1940 model with a body made of a brand new plastic called Plexiglas.

In addition to new materials, there were product innovations. Cars like the Crosley are proof that Detroit thought of down-sizing long before any "energy crunch." Crosley, of Cincinnati, Ohio, started small in corporate size and product dimensions. The company's 1941 convertible coupe cost $325 and had only three-and-one-half horsepower!

World War II

Suddenly, on December 7, 1941, America faced a new test. When Pearl Harbor was attacked, we had little national concept of what we could actually accomplish in time of war. That act proved to be the catalyst that produced the most energetic and inventive surge of industrial power in history.

By the time victory came in late 1945, the nation had received much of its vital war products from the auto industry. Over $30 billion dollars of materials were manufactured for military use. Detroit, Michigan and South Bend, Indiana; Willow Run, Michigan and Kenosha, Wisconsin and a hundred more towns and cities turned out trucks and artillery, shells and tanks, helmets and machine guns, as well as fighter planes and even huge four-engined bombers.

The Jeep quickly became the most versatile truck in America's arsenal. Designed by Bantam, it was built in the hundreds of thousands by Willys and Ford. It saw service in the deserts of North Africa, the mountain villages of Italy and the jungle atolls of the South Pacific. The Dodge-built command car operated behind the front lines in scores of battles. It was one of the many military vehicles, from weapons carriers to tanks, that Chrysler turned out in prodigious numbers from 1940 to 1945.

A little known vehicle designed and built by Studebaker was used as a troop carrier in the snow-covered terrain of Norway. Called the Weasel, it was a highly effective fighting machine. Its endless tracks, like most tank treads, were made in Akron, Ohio rubber plants.

Ford built thousands of fighting machines. Some were fitted with anti-tank cannon or 50-caliber machine guns. They could attain highway speeds of a mile-a-minute, despite the weight of the weaponry. A General Motors product was the amphibious DUKW that astonished German prisoners on the beaches of France during the invasion. The enemy troops were driven down the highways, over the sandy beaches and into the surf to be off-loaded, miles offshore, onto transports that carried them to U.S. prisoner of war camps. The DUKW had the ability to inflate and deflate its tires on the roll, to avoid bogging down in the loose sands of the beachheads.

Built by General Motors for use in World War II, the amphibious DUKW amazed German soldiers with its capabilities.

The Postwar Boom

With the Japanese surrender, reconversion to auto production began at a dozen plants. Gas rationing was dropped and the frantic scramble began for a share of this huge new seller's market. Most of the 1946 models a car-starved America awaited were actually face-lifted 1942 models. But, no one cared, because any new car was welcome. In 1946, all wartime wage and price controls were lifted and suddenly there was turmoil. Strikes in the steel industry made it tough on the independent automakers. Packard was forced to limit its output due to the steel shortage.

Demand was so great it appeared Detroit could make the same models indefinitely until Studebaker dropped a grenade in their laps. The South Bend, Indiana firm startled the industry by putting a car on the 1947 showroom floor that was easily a decade ahead of the field. The gag line was, "Is it going, or is it coming?" Studebaker laughed all the way to the bank for several years after its bold move. Detroit was also impressed by the first Nylon tire introduced in 1947 by Goodyear. They rapidly became original equipment.

Studebaker was the first marque to bring out all-new postwar styling. Charles Walter brought his 1948 Champion coupe to Akron from Niles, Michigan.

Golden Age of the American Car

The Chryslers for 1947 included a glamorous model dubbed the Town & Country. Much of the car was handmade in an Arkansas furniture factory before going to the assembly line in Detroit.

Over 100 million cars had been built in America by now. Still new makes entered the market. Henry Kaiser switched from victory ships to a pleasing new full-size car that carried his name. The Tucker appeared briefly, as did the Davis, the Playboy and the Keller. The little Crosley was sold in the Macy's department store's appliance department.

Some General Motors brands switched to V-8 engines in 1949. Even with a V-8, the top-of-the-line Oldsmobile 98 cost only $2,361, but remember that $75 a week was a good wage then! Packard survived the war, building new products with modern-sounding model names like the 1954 Patrician. It carried the last straight eight the company would use, a nine-main bearing power plant developing 210 horsepower.

The last Packard to use a straight eight engine was the 1954 model. This one, a Patrician, belongs to Bob Zimmerman of Akron, Ohio.

Chevrolet developed several models from concept vehicles seen at auto shows. The Corvette was one. Another was the striking 1955 Chevrolet Nomad, now considered the station wagon of choice among Chevrolet collectors. Back then, the lack of four-doors hurt its sales. Closing out a legend born in 1955, Ford ended the brief era of the two-seat Thunderbird with the stunning 1957 model. Sales tripled when the so-called "Squarebird" was offered starting in 1958. It had seating for four passengers.

The National Highway Act became law in 1956 and $2 billion dollars would be spent in just the next few years to develop an Interstate Highways network. American Motors, the firm that descended from the Nash and Hudson companies, did well in the late 1950s with compact, gas-saving cars. In 1961, the company sold 442,000 cars and nearly took third rank on the nationwide sales chart. General Motors took a brief fling in the volatile market for early 1960s small cars, producing such gems as the Chevrolet Corvair, Pontiac Tempest, Buick Special and Oldsmobile F-85 Cutlass. Then, 29-cents-a-gallon gas in the mid-1960s dried up the demand. Larger intermediate-sized cars took the place of compacts.

In 1964, Ford looked closely at its Falcon and decided it needed a home on the range. Totally restyled, it became the Mustang and a legend. The original 1964-1/2 thru 1966-style Mustang convertible looks as contemporary today as it did when conceived almost 30 years ago.

Advent of the Muscle Car

In the 1960s, a movement that had begun in the '50s with the Chrysler 300 high-performance model reached full flower. The muscle cars went beyond that old idea of the biggest engine block in the lightest chassis. They reached sophisticated levels of handling and braking as well as sheer speed. All manufacturers turned out muscle cars. The 1967 Dodge Coronet R/T came with 440 cubic inches and developed 375 horsepower. Needless to say, it could move! The Pontiac GTO, introduced in 1964, started another series of good-looking and sporty models. They developed a cult of "goat" lovers, as the GTO is affectionately called.

Ford Motor Company and Carroll Shelby made a series of Mustang derivatives that were popular in the 1960s and which are much sought after today. But even the standard factory issue 1969 Boss Mustang came with a massive 429-cubic-inch V-8.

When it came out, the Mustang became the best-selling new car in the history of American automobiles. This 1966 ragtop belongs to David Bowsher of Tallmadge, Ohio.

America's original muscle car was the 1964 Pontiac GTO, characterized by this convertible version owned by Gerry Gaskill, of Wadsworth, Ohio.

New Foreign Competition

We enjoyed our sporty muscle cars into the early 1970s when gasoline was still cheap. About that time, folk singer Bob Dylan was crooning "the times they are a-changing." The reality of those lyrics struck home dramatically with the OPEC oil embargo of 1973. The days of our thirsty turnpike cruisers were clearly numbered, even if we didn't realize it immediately.

While buyer and carmaker alike were fascinated with opera windows, quartz clocks and stereo sound, the growing Japanese auto industry had been concentrating on economical performance and superb fit and finish. This spelled value to the American consumer and import car sales soared along with the price of gas. Suddenly we had to accept the fact that "Yankee ingenuity" was not something confined to our native shores. Detroit had to redefine and redesign the American auto.

A new generation of vehicles combining economy, superb handling and advanced styling has been developed in the last 20 years. It was no easy order. In the period since those chaotic days of 1973 our domestic automakers have accomplished a feat bordering on a miracle. This gives us something to celebrate as we mark the 100th year since the earliest rumblings of the American auto industry.

The Challenge of the Future

We can take pride in the fact that today, more than ever before, Detroit seems fit to face the challenge of the future. The ability of free Americans to create and sustain industry, to produce profits for shareholders, to ensure careers for their children and to make products that will enhance the quality of life across the nation and the world seems to have proven itself in the auto industry. Thomas Jefferson once wrote: "Where there is no vision, the people perish." Now, more than ever, is the time for vision, for daring. The second century of the American automobile is just around the corner, and it will be very different from the first. Goodyear Tire & Rubber Company strongly believes that in this new global market, this industry, this generation of leaders, these American men and women will have the vision to endure and to prevail in that new world ahead.

(Editor's note: This story was edited from the text that Bob Stubenrauch prepared for Goodyear Tire & Rubber Company's "Century of the Auto" pageant held in Akron, Ohio in 1986. It was first printed in The BEST OF OLD CARS with permission of Goodyear Tire & Rubber Company. Bob Stubenrauch is the author of THE FUN OF OLD CARS, RUNABOUTS AND ROADSTERS and RESTORE and DRIVE COLLECTIBLE CARS of POSTWAR AMERICA.)

Goodyear Tire & Rubber Company sponsored a salute to the "Century of the Automobile" at its Akron, Ohio headquarters in 1986.

The "Century of the Automobile" pageant was held at Goodyear's technical center in Akron, Ohio.

Naturally, the Goodyear blimp was there to give VIPs a bird's-eye view of the unique automotive show.

Charlotte Maier of Massillon, Ohio brought this 1927 Kissel Gold Bug Speedster, made in Hartford, Wisconsin, to the Goodyear-sponsored exhibition.

1893-1902
Decade of Dreams

The first decade of the American car is filled with machines named after the inventive geniuses who envisioned what was to come. They converted buggies and bicycles into automobiles, powering them with gas, electric or steam. No rules, formats or industry standards bridled their thinking. Some of these men were the earliest automotive enthusiasts. They networked and traveled extensively, here and abroad, in quest of ideas. Many took part in contests or races that put their inventions to the test. Captions in this section sketch the people, places, dates and events of this "Decade of Dreams." Toward the end of the section we find hints of the automaker's transition from tinkerer to industrialist.

Various dates are sometimes attributed to the earliest American automobiles. The first Duryea is often called an 1893 vehicle, although Charles Duryea long maintained that it was first driven in 1892. During the Selden Patent Case in 1905, Henry Nadig testified that he drove his car a dozen times in 1891, but had no hard proof of this. Elwood P. Haynes often claimed his car was the first, although it didn't run until July 4, 1894. Rather than speculate about who came first, this review starts with four cars that were built and operated by 1893 and continues from there.

Duryea. *Charles S. and J. Frank Duryea started the first Duryea in Springfield, Massachusetts. After Charles moved to Peoria, Illinois, his brother completed the car and drove it in September 1893. Sometimes considered the first U.S. production vehicle, the 1893 Duryea can be seen at the Smithsonian Institution.*

Black. *Blacksmith Charles H. Black built his first car after driving a friend's European Benz. The project began in Indianapolis, Indiana during 1891 and was finished in 1892 or 1893. This makes it among the oldest cars in America. The car survives in the Indianapolis Children's Museum.*

Schloemer-Toepfer. *Gottfried Schloemer and Frank Toepfer are said to have dreamed up their car while polishing off a bucket of beer. So, naturally, the two-stroke gasoline-engined buggy was built in Milwaukee, Wisconsin. In fact, it still exists in the city's public museum. It's the only car the two men made.*

Nadig. *Gasoline engine builder Henry Nadig, of Allentown, Pennsylvania, fitted a one-cylinder motor with two flywheels to this wagon-like vehicle. It developed two horsepower at 600-800 rpm and may have been operated several times in 1891, although there are no records or patents to go by. This vehicle is still in existence today.*

1894 Balzer. *The bicycle-like Balzer was built by Stephen M. Balzer of Bronx, N.Y. A prototype of the car is in the Smithsonian Institution today. It has a three-cylinder radial engine, constant-mesh transmission and tiller steering.*

1894 Haynes-Apperson. *Elwood P. Haynes of Kokomo, Indiana, was the inventor of stainless steel and claimed for years to have invented the first U.S. car. Built in the Apperson brothers' Riverside Machine Shop, the one-cylinder vehicle had a spur gear transmission, friction differential and tiller steering. It was first driven on the Fourth of July in 1894.*

1894 Lewis. *George W. Lewis constructed his first automobile to enter the CHICAGO TIMES-HERALD contest. It incorporated a friction-drive mechanism he invented. After the 1895 race, Lewis built engines, some of which were used in other early cars. The Lewis Motor Vehicle Company operated through 1900 in Philadelphia, Pennsylvania, then disappeared.*

1895 Ames. *Built for the CHICAGO TIMES-HERALD contest in November 1895, the Ames resembled a buggy riding on two bicycles. It was constructed by a mechanic from Owatonna, Minnesota for A.C. Ames of Chicago, Illinois. He didn't complete the car until a month after the race.*

1895 Spahr. *Built by machinist Otto Spahr, of Millersburg, Ohio, this well-constructed car reflects the skill and ingenuity of the "little guy" in America. It had a water-cooled engine, friction transmission and rear differential. Spahr did not have the means to mass-produce his creation.*

1895 Morris & Salom. *Henry G. Morris and Pedro G. Salom applied for a patent to build an electric car on January 19, 1894. Their Electrobat II competed in the CHICAGO TIMES-HERALD race. It was the most sophisticated electric of the day. Morris & Salom made electrics for taxicab fleet service in New York City and Philadelphia, Pennsylvania.*

1895 Hartley Steam. *This early four-passenger car was yet another entrant in the CHICAGO TIMES-HERALD contest. It was a steamer that could utilize gasoline, coal or fuel oil to fire its burner. The Hartley Power Supply Company, of Chicago, Illinois, survived until 1899.*

1896 Riker. *This machine was constructed in the same year that a Riker-built electric racer beat a passel of gas-powered cars in the Narragansett Park Race in Rhode Island. His racer did a mile in 63 seconds. Andrew L. Riker planned his first car in 1884 and motorized an English tricycle three years later. He formed the Riker Electric Motor Company, of Brooklyn, New York, in 1888. It moved to Elizabethport, New Jersey in 1899. A year later, he sold his business to the Electric Vehicle Company.*

1896 Duryea. *The Duryea Motor Wagon Company was organized in Springfield, Massachusetts during 1895. Two Duryeas went to England for the 1896 London-to-Brighton Run. Frank Duryea finished first in one of them. The same year, 13 vehicles patterned after the winning car were built. This was the first example of mass-production of automobiles in the United States.*

1896 King. *Chicago machinist A.W. King built gas-powered horseless carriages as a sideline. They had tiller steering and wagon-like wheels. At least a half-dozen were ordered and King had to lease space in a factory to start building them.*

1896 Winton. *Alexander Winton is said to have lit the spark that got the American automobile industry going. His first car, of 1896, was an experimental one-cylinder. A year later, he formed Winton Motor Carriage Company in Cleveland, Ohio. By 1899, Winton was selling 100 cars per year. The firm survived until 1924.*

1897 Anthony. *Earle C. Anthony became famous for selling luxury cars to movie stars. As a young man, he built this electric car that could do eight miles per hour. Anthony claimed to have opened the first gas station in his native Los Angeles. He also brought the first neon sign to America, after meeting Claude Neon in Paris.*

1897 Haynes-Apperson. *Back in Kokomo, Indiana, Elwood P. Haynes and the Apperson brothers kept working their "day jobs," but continued to build a few automobiles each year. This handsome four-passenger car was among them. It pre-dates the organization of the Haynes-Apperson Automobile Company during 1898.*

1897 Cross Steam. *Alonzo T. Cross made Rhode Island's first automobile, as well as some first-class writing instruments. This car was created in his pencil factory, in Providence, between late 1896 and 1897. Two engines were prepared for it. The larger was a six-horsepower job that gave a six miles per hour top speed.*

1897 Stanley. *Identical twins F.O. and F.E. Stanley looked alike and thought alike. Their first successful steamer was built in Watertown, Massachusetts during 1897, although they had tried and failed 10 years earlier in Maine. They owned a photographic equipment company, but by 1898, they would build and sell three cars, putting them on their way to a new career.*

1898 Sperry Electric. *This electric carriage was put together by Elmer A. Sperry before he formed a company that built cars in 1899, 1900 and 1901. A Cleveland, Ohio inventor who experimented with arc lamps and electric mining equipment, Sperry won a gold medal at the 1900 Paris Exposition for his automotive ventures.*

1898 Columbia. *Over 300 types of electrics were built prior to World War II. Pope Manufacturing Company, builder of the Columbia, was formed at Waterford, Connecticut in 1896. The firm hoped to become the dominant force in the fledgling auto industry by making taxis. As early as 1899, over 2,000 cabs were made by Columbia Automobile Company.*

1898 Baker Electric. *"It outsells other electrics because it outclasses them," said Walter C. Baker's ads. This inventive genius produced his autos in Cleveland, Ohio between 1898 and 1916. Thomas Edison's first car was a Baker Electric and some automotive historians believe that Baker introduced the use of Cord tires on automobiles in 1900.*

1898 Specialty Electric. *The Specialty Carriage Company of Cincinnati, Ohio was primarily a manufacturer of horse-drawn vehicles. In 1898, it received an order to build 100 electric-powered taxicabs for the Electric Vehicle Company of New York City. Half were broughams and half were hansom cabs.*

1899 Blimline. *Sinking Springs, Pennsylvania was home to just one automaker. Sebastian Blimline, who built carriages there, manufactured his 1-1/2 horsepower auto-buggy between 1898 and 1899. It carried two passengers at two speeds: three or 10 miles per hour.*

1899 Packard Model A. *James Ward Packard didn't like his 1898 Winton and went off to build his own car. The Ohio Automobile Company in the city of Warren, Ohio resulted. The original Model A was completed on November 6, 1899. By 1900, Packard had made 50 cars and launched his firm.*

1899 Locomobile Steamer. Early "Locos" were made in Watertown, Massachusetts during 1899 and 1900 using bicycle frames, chain-drive, tiller steering and inefficient steam engines. Later, the company moved to Bridgeport, Connecticut. It improved its product and switched to gasoline engines. Locomobile lasted until 1929 as an outstanding American automaker.

1899 Waverley Electric Model 18. A merger of Chicago's American Electric Vehicle Company and the Indiana Bicycle Company led to the manufacture of Waverleys in Indianapolis. The company went through many transitions, but kept building a wide variety of cars until 1916.

1900 Knox Three-wheeler. *Frank Duryea prompted Harry A. Knox to build cars in Springfield, Massachusetts. Fifteen three-wheelers were made during 1900. A four-wheeler came in 1902 and the air-cooled "Waterless Knox" appeared in 1903. Knox then left the company, which continued making bigger and fancier cars until 1914.*

1900 McKay Steamer. *Produced in Lawrence, Massachusetts by the Stanley Manufacturing Company (No relation to Stanley Steamers.) the McKay Steamer sold for $1,800. Some were shown at the first American Automobile Show at New York City's Madison Square Garden in 1900. About 25 were made before the company switched to making sewing machines.*

1900 Pennington. *Edward Joel Pennington promoted many visionary ideas, but finished very few of them. Several of the companies he formed in Wisconsin, New York and Pennsylvania built a handful of prototype cars. This one had a cow-catcher to clear traffic, since there was more livestock on the roads than automobiles.*

1900 St. Louis. *Automaker George Dorris and musical instrument maker John L. French formed St. Louis Motor Carriage Company in 1899. By 1900, they had built 130 cars. The single-cylinder model of 1900 had a piano box body, bicycle tires and tiller steering. "Rigs that Run" was the company slogan. Between 1905 and 1907, St. Louis cars were actually made in Peoria, Illinois by the same firm.*

1901 Gasmobile. *At the turn-of-the-century, gas, steam and electric power vied for dominance in the auto industry. This make, built in New York (1899-1900) and Marion, New Jersey (1900-1902) made clear which camp it was in. By November 1901, production hit 140 cars. A year earlier, the Gasmobile won every contest for gasoline cars at the first New York Automobile Show.*

1901 Waverley Electric. *This was the only electric model made by Colonel Alexander Pope, an Indianapolis, Indiana bicycle manufacturer who built many cars bearing his name. It sprung from the 1898 merger of Chicago's American Electric Vehicle Company and the Indiana Bicycle Company, which evolved through the American Bicycle Company (1900) into the International Motor Car Company (1901-1903). This 20a surrey was one of three models. The name Pope-Waverley was adopted for the firm in 1904.*

1901 Mobile Steamer. *Mobiles were built by a Tarrytown, New York company that evolved from the purchase of the Stanley patents by two partners who soon split up. John Brisben Walker formed Mobile Steam and Amzi Lorenzo Barber started Locomobile. About 600 Mobile Steamers were built from 1900 to 1903. One of them inspired the early motoring song "My Mobile Gal" for the Broadway play "The Belle of Bohemia."*

1901 Curved Dash Oldsmobile Model R. *In spring 1901, a disastrous fire gutted Olds Motor Works. A single prototype Curved Dash model survived the inferno. Ransom E. Olds went on to rebuild the factory and make the Curved Dash Oldsmobile the most famous of early American cars.*

1902 Rambler. *A partner in the successful American Bicycle Company, Thomas B. Jeffery experimented with a one-cylinder car that caught media attention at the 1900 Chicago and New York auto shows. This $750 Rambler went into production in 1902. Soon Jeffery was selling 124 per month.*

1902 Thomas. *The E.R. Thomas Motor Company was formed during 1902 in Buffalo, New York. It took over the Buffalo Automobile & Auto-Bi Company and marketed versions of its Buffalo Senior and the Model 17 and Model 18 Thomas cars. They were both one-cylinder, eight-horsepower machines sharing a 78-inch wheelbase. By 1904, the famous Thomas Flyer appeared with a three-cylinder engine. Thereafter, the firm made fours and sixes and continued in business through 1917.*

1902 National Electric. *L.S. Dow and Philip Goetz founded the National Automobile & Electric Company in 1900. The cars they built were said to be "For those who find no pleasure in mechanical labor." Eight models were marketed by the Indianapolis, Indiana firm in 1902. They ranged from an $850 runabout to a $1,100 dos-a-dos. Nicknamed "Electrobiles," the vehicles were simple in design. The company claimed that one 1902 National ran 118 miles on a single charge.*

1902 Haynes-Apperson. *Elwood P. Haynes always down-played the role of the Apperson brothers in his automotive ventures. In late 1901, they split up and he started making Appersons. However, the Haynes-Apperson name was also continued through 1904. The 1902 line included three models with two-cylinder engines. This eight-horsepower runabout for $1,200 was the entry-level offering. A phaeton ($1,500) and a surrey ($1,800) were offered with 12-horsepower motors.*

Early Auto Slogans

Abbott-Detroit - The One Perfect Car

A.B.C. - As Simple as You Can Guess to Operate

Acme - From Steel Bar to Finished Car

Adams-Farwell - It Spins Like a Top

Allen - Wonderful Power; the King of the Hill Climbers

American - Miles of Smiles

Anderson - The Season's Most Enchanting Car

Auburn - Once an Owner, Always a Friend

Austin - A Car to Run Around In

Beaver - A High-Class Car

Beggs - Made a Little Better Than Seems Necessary

Buick - When Better Automobiles are Built, Buick Will Build Them

Cadillac - The Standard of the World

Cartercar - No Clutch to Slip, No Gears to Strip

Chandler - Car of the Year

Chrysler Airflow - The Beauty of Nature Itself

Cleveland - The Car Without a Weak Spot

Cole - The World's Safest Car

Columbia - The Gem of the Highway

Commonwealth - The Car with the Foundation

Continental Beacon - The Lowest-Priced Full-Sized Car in the World

Daniels - The Distinguished Car to the Discriminating

DeVaux - A Jewel for Beauty

Diana - The Easiest Steering Car in America

Dodge - The American Beauty

Dorris - Built Up to a Standard, Not Down to a Price

Driggs - Built with the Precision of Ordnance

Duesenberg - The World's Champion Automobile

DuPont - The Car That Makes an Instant Appeal

Durant - Just a Real Good Car

Elgin - World's Champion Light 6

Elmore - The Car That Has No Valves

Empire - The Little Aristocrat

Falcon-Knight - America's Finest Type of Motor

Flint - The Sensation of the Year

Ford - There's a Ford in Your Future

Gas Au Lec - The Simple Car

Gearless - A Common Sense Car with No Tender or Delicate Parts

Glide - Ride in a Glide, Then Decide

Handley-Knight - For the Fine Car Owner Who Drives from Choice

Hanover - Saves Money Every Mile

Haynes-Apperson - America's First Car

Hudson - Look for the White Triangle

Jackson - No Hill Too Steep, No Sand Too Deep

Jewett - In All the World, No Car Like This

King - The Car of No Regrets

Kissel - The Custom-Built Car

Kline - The Ace of the Highway

Leach - The Master Creation of the Year

Liberty - All the World Loves a Winner

Lincoln - Get Behind the Wheel

Marmon - The Easiest Riding Car in the World

Martin - The Little Brother of the Aeroplane

Maxwell - Perfectly Simple - Simply Perfect

Maytag - The Hill Climber

Metz - The Car You'll be Proud to Own

Moore - The World's Biggest Little Automobile

Nash - Leads the World in Motor Car Value

National - The All-Ball-Bearing Car

Oldsmobile - Nothing to Watch but the Road

Packard - Ask the Man Who Owns One

Paige - The Most Beautiful Car in America

Pierce-Arrow - Pride of Its Makers Makes You Proud

Pilot - The Car Ahead

Pope-Toledo - The Quiet, Mile-a-Minute Car

Premier - The Aluminum 6 with Magnetic Gear Shift

Reo - The Gold Standard of Values

Rickenbacker - A Car Worthy of its Name

Roamer - America's Smartest Car

Sears - The Businessman's Car

Sheridan - The Complete Car

Standard - A Powerful Car

Star - Worth the Money

Stephens - 'Tis a Great Car

Stevens-Duryea - There Is No Better Motor Car

Studebaker - The Automobile with a Reputation Behind It

Templar - The Superfine Small Car

Vaughn - Made in the Carolinas

Westcott - The Car with a Longer Life

1903 Cadillac. Later models of the marque were advertised as "The Standard of the World."

1903-1912
Oaks From Little Acorns

The second decade of American cars left a lasting imprint on history. It saw the formation of Ford, General Motors and Chrysler predecessor Maxwell-Briscoe. Other long-lasting nameplates such as Studebaker and Rambler (sire of AMC) originated, too. Cars continued to reflect many design variations and power source choices, although four-wheelers and gas-powered vehicles gained the greatest popularity. The steering wheel became the directional control mechanism of choice. Mass production techniques were developed and Cadillac championed the standardization of parts. Other important advances included electric lighting and starting, multi-cylinder engines and closed-body cars. Sales grew by leaps and bounds. Prices on some cars, most notably the Model T Ford, dropped towards the range of the common man. The auto trade was branching out into a solid industry.

1903 Cadillac. Henry M. Leland made marine engines in Detroit, Michigan before teaming with Henry Ford to build cars. Leland favored precision engineering over Ford's concentration on speedy production. They split up and LeLand formed Cadillac. "A look ought to tell you why," he advertised in 1903.

1903 Ford Model A. Henry Ford's original Model A was made in a two-story wooden factory in Detroit. The genius machinist made his first car in 1896, but the 1903 model was the first product of Ford Motor Company. He started his firm after quitting as chief engineer at Detroit Automobile Company

1903 Winton. *By 1903, Alexander Winton had been building cars in Cleveland, Ohio for eight years. They were so reliable that Dr. H. Nelson Jackson and his chauffeur drove one from San Francisco to New York. These two-cylinder, 20 horsepower vehicles sold for $2,500 with a detachable tonneau. Sales hit a new record of 850 units in 1903.*

1903 Franklin. *H.H. Franklin was an automotive pioneer who built only air-cooled cars. As early as 1902, he marketed a four-cylinder model with a transverse-mounted gas engine that cranked on the right side. The company was located in Syracuse, New York.*

1904 Locomobile Model D. *Locomobile started as a steam carmaker. The Model D was the firm's fanciest 1904 model, selling at prices from $4,000 to $5,000. It had an 86-inch wheelbase and a four-cylinder T-head engine. "Easily the best built car in America," was its slogan.*

1904 Columbia. *Columbia was actually a trade name of Hartford, Connecticut's Electric Vehicle Company. Early Columbias were created for city taxicab service. By 1904, the company produced a wide range of models from an $850 electric runabout to a $5,000 European-style gas-powered touring car. Columbias were among the most advanced electrics of the day.*

1904 Packard Model L. *This 1904 model introduced the flat hood and distinctive radiator design that became early Packard trademarks. With its light aluminum-over-wood body, the Model L could do 40 miles per hour. It had a 22-horsepower four-cylinder engine of 241.7 cubic-inches.*

1904 Buick Model B. *Plumber David Dunbar Buick invented the process to make white porcelain bathtubs. He used his profits to develop a car with a two-cylinder valve-in-head engine. Buick made 16 cars in 1903 and 37 in 1904. Then W.C. Durant purchased Buick in late 1904, and made it the cornerstone of his new General Motors.*

1905 Glide Model A. *J.B. Bartholomew, of Peoria, Illinois was a maker of coffee and peanut roasters. He launched the Glidemobile in 1903. An advance introduced in the 1905 models was mounting the power plant to the chassis, independent of the body, for a smoother ride.*

1905 Maxwell. *The "good little Maxwell" was a predecessor of the Chrysler. Benjamin Briscoe felt uncomfortable with his investment in Buick. Then, engineer Jonathan D. Maxwell came along. The partners built 823 cars in 1905 and 100,000 by 1917. Eight years later, after a financial downturn, Chrysler improved and renamed the Maxwell.*

1905 Thomas Flyer. *The Thomas Flyer was made in Buffalo, N.Y. For 1905, the company released its biggest and most expensive models. Top-of-the-line Flyers had a 60-horsepower six, a 124-inch wheelbase and $6,000 price.*

1905 Peerless Model 9. *Packard, Pierce and Peerless were the famed "Three Ps" of the infant auto industry. Peerless stressed quality over quantity. The Model 9 had a 284-cubic-inch four-cylinder engine developing 24-horsepower. With 18 coats of hand-brushed lacquer finish and silver fittings, the Cleveland-built Peerless was truly a prestige automobile.*

1906 Rambler. *"The Right Car at the Right Price" Rambler advertised in 1906 when a new series of four-cylinder cars was introduced. They joined a quartet of two-cylinder models to form a solid product line of vehicles priced from $800 to $3,000. At this time, the Kenosha, Wisconsin firm was America's number two automaker.*

1906 Winton Model K. *Scottish engineer Alexander Winton built this big $2,500 four-cylinder car in Cleveland, Ohio. Its 354.4-cubic-inch engine was rated for 40- to 50-horsepower. The first car to cross the U.S. was a Winton.*

1906 National Model E. *National made both gasoline and electric cars in Indianapolis, Indiana, but electrics were on their way out in 1906. So, the 60-horsepower Model E was introduced with a 121-inch wheelbase and $4,000 price tag. It inspired a lot of "National pride."*

1906 Pope-Hartford Model L. *Colonel Albert Pope's boldest venture in auto making was a splendid, high speed car. It had a 25- to 30-horsepower four and a 102-inch wheelbase. The touring car shown and the run-about were both $2,750 and a limousine was $1,000 more.*

1907 Cadillac Model K. *Henry M. LeLand learned precision manufacturing under Samuel Colt. The single-cylinder Model K was one example. In 1908, this car took the Dewar Trophy for Cadillac by winning the Royal Automobile Club's "Standardization test" in England.*

1907 Ford Model K. *A racing version of the "K" set a 24-hour speed record by covering 1,135 miles at an average of 47.2 miles per hour at Ormond Beach, Florida. It came as a runabout or touring at $2,500. The big 405-cubic-inch six produced 40 horsepower. Henry Ford became president of Ford Motor Company in 1906.*

1907 Stevens-Duryea Model U. Frank Duryea designed this car as an employee of the Stevens Firearms Company. It was a $3,500 light six. The 309.5-cubic-inch engine developed 30 to 35 horsepower. "There is no better motor car" was the sales slogan. Top speed for this car was 56 miles per hour. It was considered quite fast for its era.

1907 Lambert Model F. John William Lambert, of Anderson, Indiana built a three-wheel gas buggy as early as 1891, but his first production model came in 1906. The Model F was the costliest of five models at $3,000. The engine was a 40 horsepower four and it had a 106-inch wheelbase.

1908 Buick Model 10. *This most famous "little white Buick" was a hot car for its day. It won many road races and 8,800 customers. Selling for $900, it had a 165 cubic-inch four developing 22.5 horsepower.*

1908 Pierce-Arrow 60. *This fabulous car cost $6,500. It had a 60 horsepower six and a huge 135-inch wheelbase. Although the "Great Arrow" was known for its vibration-free operation, it was among the most powerful and speedy cars of 1908.*

1908 Overland. John N. Willys ordered 47 Overlands to sell. They never arrived, so he went to the factory in Indianapolis, Indiana and found things in disarray. Willys took over the firm, setting up a huge tent to build 465 cars. By 1909, Willys-Overland moved to Toledo, Ohio. The driver of this 1908 touring car is dressed up as Saint Nicholas to deliver Christmas presents.

1908 Brush. Known as a good hill-climber, the Brush was a $500 car that could do 35 miles per hour. One- and two-cylinder models were offered only in 1908. All other Brush cars were single-cylinder autos. Alanson P. Brush was also a consulting engineer for General Motors.

1909 Model T Ford. *Almost 20 years after building his first auto, Henry Ford launched his affordable "dream car." It was a simple machine that the common man could purchase, because of Ford's low-cost production methods. By 1927, Model T Ford sales hit 15,000,000.*

1909 Inter-State Model 28. *The Inter-State was made in Muncie, Indiana from 1909 to 1919. A 35- to 40-horsepower four was used in all 1909 models. They all had a 112-inch wheelbase and $1,750 price tag.*

1909 Stanley Steamer. *After the Stanley twins sold their early steam car patents they formed Stanley Motor Carriage Company in Newton, Massachusetts and began production in the spring of 1901. Their coffin-nosed cars were fast and famous for it. The streamlined "Woggle-bug" race car went 127.66 miles per hour at Daytona Beach, Florida in 1906. The Stanleys pulled out of racing in 1908. The 1909 Model R was a 20-horsepower roadster on a 112-inch wheelbase. It sold for about $1,400.*

1909 Thomas Flyer Model K. *Built in Buffalo, New York by E.R. Thomas, the Flyer was famous for winning the 1908 New York-to-Paris Race. With a 784-cubic-inch six the 3,600-pound car could do 70 miles per hour.*

ix Runabout.

1910 Chadwick Six. *Under 300 Chadwicks were ever made. Lee Sherman Chadwick built a supercharged six as early as 1907. The production model of 1908-1910 used a 706.9-cubic-inch six to generate 70- to 75-horsepower. Chain-drive was an unusual feature for a car of this era.*

1910 Simplex 50. *Simplex autos were made in New York City. They gave "jack rabbit" performance with a 597-cubic-inch, 50-horsepower four-cylinder engine and four-speed transmission. Double camshafts and two spark plugs per cylinder added to the get-up-and-go of these big motor cars.*

1910 Palmer-Singer. Henry Palmer made barrels and Charles A. Singer was heir to the Singer Sewing Machine fortune. Together, they began selling large, powerful cars to New York City clients. In 1908, they formed Palmer-Singer to build their own automobile. This 1910 Palmer-Singer Model LXII Sixty-sixty Toy Tonneau originally sold for $3,500. It has a 127-inch wheelbase and 616-cubic-inch 60-horsepower six. Once part of the Harrah's Automobile Collection and said to be the favorite tour car of William F. Harrah, current owner Walter E. Cunny entered the car in the 1984 Great American Race.

1910 Stevens-Duryea. The Model Y was Stevens-Duryea's largest and most powerful 1910 model with a 142-inch wheelbase and 54-horsepower six. The touring sold for $4,000, the limousine for $5,000. "There is no better motor car," the Chicopee Falls, Massachusetts company often advertised. Production averaged about 100 vehicles per year at this time.

1911 Detroit Electric Model 17. *This company built an immense variety of electric-powered cars from 1907 to 1939. It was the longest-lasting electric vehicle maker. The Model 17 was an under-slung roadster on a 96-inch wheelbase with a $2,700 price tag. Chainless, direct shaft-drive was introduced this year.*

1911 Alco 60. *Power, strength and simple construction were features of the 60-horsepower six built by American Locomotive Company of Providence, Rhode Island. The 578.5-cubic-inch engine could propel the 4,125-pound car to 85 miles per hour. Priced $6,000 to $6,750, ads said the Alco had "perfect balance and fitness for conquest of all roads."*

1911 Mercer 35. *Trenton, New Jersey was the home of the Mercer, one of America's favorite early sports cars. The T-head raceabout introduced for 1911 had a 34-horsepower 300-cubic-inch four-cylinder engine, a three-speed transmission and a 116-inch wheelbase. It sold for $2,250. Mercer T-heads won five of the six big road races in 1911.*

1911 Oldsmobile Limited. *The Oldsmobile Limited was so big it had double-level running boards and 42-inch tires. A 707-cubic-inch six of 60-horsepower could push the monster to 75 miles per hour. "A new standard of luxury in motoring" said the catalog. Only 310 Limiteds were built.*

1912 Packard 6-48. *Packard switched to a six and shaft drive to create a fast car. With a top speed of 80 miles per hour and 30 second 0-to-60 acceleration, the "48" filled the bill. The 525 cubic-inch engine developed 74 brake horsepower. Prices ran $5,000 to $6,550.*

1912 Marmon Model 32. *The Marmon Wasp that took the first Indy 500 was a racing version of the Model 32. Howard C. Marmon enhanced his reputation with his T-head four of 317 cubic inches and 32 horsepower. Introduced in 1909, the speedy Marmon model lasted until 1918.*

1912 Winton Model 17. *Another Winton among the outstanding early American cars was the "17." It had a 477-cubic-inch six that produced 60- to 70-horsepower. Top speed was an impressive 74 miles per hour despite its long 136-inch wheelbase and 4,000-pounds weight.*

1912 Pullman Model 6-60. *Pullman autos were built in York, Pennsylvania. The 60-horsepower model was a 1912 development. A Pullman won the famous Fairmont Park Road Race in Philadelphia in both 1910 and 1911. The Model 6-60 was on a large 138-inch wheelbase and priced from $3,200 to $5,500.*

In the Ford kitchen . . . this little trial engine sputtered into life

IT HAPPENED far back—in the very early 1890's. In the kitchen of his Detroit home, a young engineer, named Henry Ford, was testing a principle of the internal combustion engine.

His apparatus, clamped to the kitchen sink, was a piece of one-inch gas pipe, reamed out for a cylinder—the flywheel, a hand-wheel from a lathe. Gasoline was fed from an oil cup. A wire connected to the kitchen light furnished the spark.

He spun the flywheel. Flame came from the exhaust, the sink shook and the trial engine was running under its own power Mr.

Ford was satisfied. He put the engine aside. It had served its purpose. His idea was proved.

But he did not stop to applaud himself. "The man who thinks he has done something," Mr. Ford once said, "hasn't even started." His mind was already stirring with thoughts of a new and larger engine for transportation use.

Just ahead lay the pioneering which was to produce the Ford automobile of world-wide use. Ahead lay the creation of the first industrial assembly line, hundreds of inventions and improvements, the building of 30,000,000 low-cost motor cars and trucks to

serve the needs of *all* the people.

Today, at Ford Motor Company the pioneering still goes forward. New methods, new materials, new devices are continually being developed. You don't hear about many of them, because Ford assignments now are military.

But one day the story of this modern pioneering *can* be told. It will be told, you may be sure, through the medium of Ford, Mercury and Lincoln cars so advanced in both style and engineering that new millions will seek to own them —for comfort, for smartness, for reliability, and for economy.

FORD MOTOR COMPANY

During World War II, Ford Motor Company ran a series of interesting advertisements that spotlighted the automaker's contributions to American history. This one shows an engine that Henry Ford invented in the kitchen of his Detroit home during the very early 1890s. The copy in the advertisement compared Henry Ford's pioneering work with experiments that the company was conducting for the military during the war years and suggested that these would lead to future advances in automotive technology.

1913-1922
Years of Fulfillment

By 1913, a Sunday drive in the family car was no longer a novelty. The industry was building as many cars per year as it had made in its history. An opinion survey of 1916 would indicate that Americans wished to achieve the goal of one automobile per citizen. As factories across the nation cranked out vast numbers of cars, that ratio began to look realistic. Though there was still a wide variety of manufacturers and types of cars, a trend towards uniformity of design could be seen. Dark-colored touring cars powered by gasoline engines lined the streets of America. Sales of steamers and electrics were dwindling. The most successful auto makers were those that built large fleets of affordable, look-alike autos that average families could buy. Thanks to the steady growth of mass production, this was an era in which countless Americans fulfilled the dream of automobile ownership.

1913 Locomobile 6-38. *This car was Locomobile's "Little Six." In 1913, it evolved into a near perfect blend of performance and mechanical sophistication. The 425.5-cubic-inch engine produced 60 brake horsepower. It had a selective four-speed transmission and 128-inch wheelbase. Prices ranged from $4,400 to $5,700.*

1913 American Underslung. *"A Car for the Discriminating Few" was the sales slogan for this racy-looking vehicle made in Indianapolis, Indiana by the company that first used the name American Motors. Its nickname came from the fact that the frame hung below the axles. Three 1913 lines all used different four-cylinder engines. Wheelbases and horsepower ratings varied: 105 inches for the 30-horsepower Scout; 118 inches for the 5-horsepower Tourist; and 140 inches for the 60-horsepower Traveler. This Traveler is from the Indianapolis Motor Speedway's "Hall of Fame" museum.*

1913 Hudson 6-54. With a top speed of 65 miles per hour, the Model 6-54 made Hudson "the world's largest producer of six-cylinder automobiles." It could get up to 58 miles per hour in 30 seconds thanks to its 421-cubic-inch engine with 54 horsepower. Hudson's Detroit factory built 6,404 cars in 1913.

1913 Abbott-Detroit. Charles Abbott started the Abbott Motor Car Company in Detroit, Michigan in 1909. Available for 1913 were two four-cylinder series, one of 40 horsepower and the other of 50 horsepower. The smaller cars had a 116-inch wheelbase, while the larger ones (like this Model 44-50 touring) had a 121-inch stance.

1914 Peerless 6-48. *Another big car of the early teens was the Peerless 6-48. It had a 4.5-inch x 6-inch bore and stroke for 570 cubic inches. This, believe it or not, was the company's "Little Six." The "Big Six" had 824 cubic inches and 60 horsepower. However, the 6-48 was smaller and lighter and really much better suited for spirited driving.*

1914 Detroit Electric. *Popular with women drivers as a city-use vehicle, the Detroit Electric had a "telephone booth" body, shaft drive and electric propulsion system good for trips of 80 miles between recharges. All 1914 models shared a 100-inch wheelbase, with prices ranging from $2,300 to $3,000. Production hit 4,669 cars in 1914, including this example that was Mrs. Henry Ford's personal car. Detroit Electrics survived until 1935, long after most electric cars were gone.*

1914 McFarlan Model T. *Founded in Connersville, Indiana in 1910, Alfred McFarlan's fine automobile was renowned for power and speed. Below the hood of the series T models was a 452-cubic-inch six capable of pushing them to 80 miles per hour.*

1914 Stutz Bearcat. *This famous early sports car was made by an Indianapolis, Indiana firm founded in 1911 to build race cars. The Bearcat name first applied to the raceabout body style, rather than the series. Bearcats came in both four- and six-cylinder series the first few years. However, the 1914 Bearcat model was offered only in the Series 4E, which was powered by a 50-horsepower four. It had a 120-inch wheelbase and $2,000 price tag.*

1915 Mercer 22-70. *"Mercer is the Steinway of the automobile world," said the Trenton, New Jersey company's ads. A 70-horsepower four-cylinder engine powered the four 1915 models. Sporting and touring models on a 130-inch wheelbase cost $3,000. The raceabout and runabout, at $2,750 and $2,900, had a 115-inch stance. They could hit 60 miles per hour.*

1915 Mitchell Special Six. *Combining Mitchell's 43.3-horsepower six with a 132-inch wheelbase made the Special an attractive package. Buyers could order the roadster or five-passenger touring for $1,895 or add $100 for a seven-passenger touring. Mitchells were built in Racine, Wisconsin.*

1915 Rauch & Lang Electric. *These high-quality electrics were built in Cleveland, Ohio between 1905 and 1920 and in Chicopee Falls, Massachusetts between 1920 and 1928. By 1915, electric car sales were beginning to decline. As a result, the company merged with Baker Motor Vehicle Company. Nine models were offered at prices from $2,600 to $4,000.*

1915 Lozier Type 82. *One of America's stellar marques, Lozier moved to Detroit, Michigan in 1910 when the "Big Six" was first introduced as the Type 51. With a 560-cubic-inch T-head motor, that 51-horsepower car could hit 80 miles per hour. The Type 82 seven-passenger touring had a 132-inch wheelbase and a $3,250 price tag.*

1916 Hudson Super Six. *The new-for-1916 Hudson made motoring history for its record-setting transcontinental run of five days, three hours and 31 minutes. Ralph Mulford drove another 102.53 miles per hour at Daytona Beach and set a record by climbing Pike's Peak in 18 minutes 24 seconds. The 289-cubic-inch engine produced 76-horsepower and came in a wide range of models selling for less than $3,000.*

1916 Brewster Coupe. *Brewster, of Long Island City, New York, was a famous carriage builder. The firm manufactured its own unique luxury cars for 10 years between 1916 and 1925. They featured Knight four-cylinder sleeve-valve engines. The 1916 coupe was an elegant, 26-horsepower car for $6,500. It had a 125-inch wheelbase.*

1916 Sun. *"The Sun Outshines Them All,"* was the motto of this Elkhart, Indiana automaker. Ex-Haynes employee Roscoe C. Hoffman designed this light six-cylinder car that was priced in the $1,000 range. It had a 116-inch wheelbase and developed 23 horsepower, although the manufacturer insisted it could produce 50 horsepower.

1916 Cole. *Cole Automobiles were manufactured in Indianapolis from 1909 to 1925. Joseph J. Cole dreamed of running the "General Motors of Indiana," but never quite made it that big. The eight-cylinder Model 8-50 of 1916 was constructed on a 127-inch wheelbase with the touring car priced at $1,785. It developed 39.2 horsepower. Up until just a few years ago, a pair of virtually new Coles were stored inside the company's old factory and still owned by the Cole family.*

1917 Pathfinder Twelve. *Pathfinders were made in Indianapolis, Indiana from 1912 to 1917. They performed outstandingly in races and long distance endurance runs. The 1917 twelve-cylinder models rode a 130-inch wheelbase and generated 60 horsepower. Models included a LaSalle touring, the Cloverleaf roadster seen here, and a Berline Limousine.*

1917 Dodge Model 30. *Not every famous American car of the teens was an expensive, powerful monster. The 35-horsepower Dodge four earned its stripes by serving well in General John Pershing's U.S. Army campaign against Mexican bandit Pancho Villa. The durable Dodges also distinguished themselves during World War I.*

1917 Haynes Light Twelve. *Bowing at the 1916 New York Automobile Show, the Haynes V-12 turned out to be a rarity. Only 650 were built through 1921. Displacing 365.3 cubic inches, the big motor was rated at a modest 36.3 ALAM-horsepower.*

1917 Marmon 34. *An exquisite example of excellent engineering, the "34" had a mostly aluminum engine and an aluminum body and radiator shell. The 340-cubic-inch 74-horsepower overhead-valve six could get the 3,295-pound Marmon from 0-to-50 miles per hour in 19 seconds. The top speed of this under-$3,000 car was 60-70 miles per hour.*

1918 Jordan Roadster. *America fell head-over-heels for Ned Jordan's "Somewhere west of Laramie" ads that painted a romantic picture of open car ownership. The $1,990 sports roadster had a 30-horsepower four. In 1919, Ned Jordan added a six-cylinder engine and nicknamed his roadster the "Playboy." It's a name that has become famous with antique car fans.*

1918 Scripps-Booth. *James Scripps-Booth made "luxurious light cars," as well as cyclecars in Detroit, Michigan. His company started in 1912. By late 1917, it became part of General Motors. The 1918 Model 639 roadster, priced at $1,245, was a 40-horsepower car on a 112-inch wheelbase.*

1918 Stephens Salient Six. *The Stephens was made in Freeport, Illinois by Moline Plow Company and named for G.A. Stephens, whose father founded the firm in 1870. For 1918, the Salient Six received a new overhead-valve 25.35-horsepower engine. Stephens built about 25,000 cars in seven years.*

1918 Studebaker "Big Six." *For 1918, Studebaker broke from its EMF origins and added the new model EG "Big Six" touring. It featured a 353.8-cubic-inch L-head engine that developed 60 horsepower at 2,000 rpm. With an attractive $1,795 price, the Big Six realized 11,757 sales.*

1919 Daniels. *"A distinguished car to the discriminating" was the Daniels sales slogan. They were built in Reading, Pennsylvania from 1916 to 1924. The 1919 Model C had a 45-horsepower eight-cylinder engine and 127-inch wheelbase. It sold for $3,750.*

1919 Mercer Sporting. *With a 70-horsepower L-head four, the Series 4 promised high performance to early sports car fans willing to spend $4,350. A Wall Street syndicate bought Mercer in 1919.*

1919 Biddle. *A fancy car associated with R. Ralston Biddle, a member of Philadelphia's high society, the Biddle was built in that Pennsylvania city from 1915 to 1922. The 1919 four-passenger touring car was priced at $2,750. It had a 23-horsepower four-cylinder engine and a 121-inch wheelbase.*

1919 Chandler. *Founded by a group of ex-Lozier employees, Chandler Motor Car Company of Cleveland, Ohio was organized to build a car similar to Lozier's highly regarded Light Six. The venture started under the name of C.A. Emise, a former Lozier sales manager, but soon took F.C. Chandler's name. The 1919 offering was a 30-horsepower model on a 123-inch wheelbase. The touring car listed for $1,795. Chandler was ultimately absorbed by Hupp Motor Car Company.*

1920 Porter. *Television fans will remember the antique "Porter" that starred in the series "My Mother th. Car." The real Porter was a quite different automobile. It was the most expensive American car of 1920. Witl its custom coach work, the price of this Bridgeport, Connecticut product exceeded $10,000. Only 36 were buil*

1920 Cunningham. *Once a builder of high quality dog carts, this Rochester, New York firm entered automaking in 1907. From the World War I era to the Roaring '20s, Cunningham made America's handsomest cars. The prices were handsome, too. It cost up to $8,100 for a 95-horsepower eight on a 142-inch wheelbase.*

1920 Apperson. *Elmer and Edgar Apperson formed their own company in 1902, after splitting with Elwood P. Haynes. They produced Appersons in Kokomo, Indiana through 1926. The best known model may have been the sporty "Jack Rabbit." The V-8 powered "Anniversary" series of 1920 was made up of five 60-horsepower cars on a 130-inch wheelbase. With prices from $4,000 to $5,500, they were not inexpensive.*

1920 Chalmers. *Hugh Chalmer's first car represented an early example of badge-engineering; it was a Thomas-Detroit with a Chalmers name badge. Then the high-paid National Cash Register Company executive went into automaking full time producing Chalmers-Detroit and Chalmers models. The 1920 Model 35-C touring sold for $1,685. It had a 45-horsepower six and a 117-inch wheelspan.*

1921 Moon 6-68. *"The Ideal American Car" was a sales pitch used by this St. Louis, Missouri company. The Model 6-68 touring sold for $2,485. It had a 68-horsepower six and 124-inch wheelbase. Moons were made from 1905 to 1929.*

1921 Ambassador Model R. *Taxicab baron John Hertz built a large, elegant car called the Ambassador from 1921-1925. It had a 136-inch wheelbase and 75-horsepower six. "The new Ambassador stands out prominently in the field of the world's finest cars," Hertz claimed.*

1921 Milburn Electric. *Selling for $2,685, the 1921 Milburn 27L Brougham featured batteries that slid out on rollers for quick replacement, rather than time-consuming re-charging. Milburns were made in Toledo, Ohio from 1914-1923. Top speed was 15 miles per hour.*

1921 Peerless Model 56. *Along with Packard and Pierce-Arrow, this marque was one of the three "P-for-prestige" early American super-cars. The Cleveland, Ohio firm had actually manufactured clothes wringers before entering automaking from 1900 to 1931. The Model 56 touring car of 1921 was a $3,230 machine with a powerful 80-horsepower eight-cylinder engine and a 125-inch wheelbase. Production for 1921 was a strong 3,500 vehicles despite the post-World War I economic recession.*

1922 Lincoln Model L. *"Get behind the wheel" was an early sales slogan for the Lincoln. Ex-Cadillac legend Henry M. Leyland founded Lincoln in 1920. By February 1922, sales had reached just 3,407 cars and the company's board of directors sold the firm to Henry Ford for $8 million. With its 60-degree V-8 and fork-and-blade connecting rods, the $3,400 Lincoln chassis was high-tech for its day.*

1922 Oakland Model 6-44. *This Pontiac, Michigan firm was founded in 1908 and originally built large, powerful cars that were known as good hill-climbers. It became part of General Motors and ultimately sired the Pontiac. The 1922 Model 6-44 was advertised as a "good mechanism" and guaranteed in writing for 15,000 miles. Duco laquer finish was first introduced by Oakland.*

1922 Velie 58. *Velies were made in Moline, Illinois from 1909 to 1929. They were very interesting and stylish cars and somewhat competitive in racing for a while. The Model 58 came with a 45-horsepower six. Open models were $1,395 and closed cars sold for $2,195.*

1922 Haynes Model 55. *Industry pioneer Elwood P. Haynes was still making automotive history in the 1920s. The "55" had an L-head six of 50-horsepower. Prices for three body styles ranged from $1,785 to $2,835. They could do 75 miles per hour.*

A Toast to Model T

● For all the jokes that Model T inspired, the memory is one of affection and respect. And that is only right.

If it would never occur to you to build a house without a garage, it is because Model T established the principle of universal ownership of automobiles.

If you drive five hundred effortless miles in a day, it is because Model T forced the building of paved highways.

And it was a symbol of the manufacturing skill and integrity to which we, ourselves, subscribe. Remember the Model T slogan: Wherever you go you see it; wherever you see it, it's going.

No other single product has had so profound an influence on every aspect of the way we live today.

Our first association with the Ford Motor Company was making body parts for Model T, in 1918. It is an association we have prized ever since and enjoy today, and lends extra warmth to our congratulations to this great Company on the occasion of its fiftieth anniversary.

The Budd Company, Philadelphia, Detroit, Gary.

**PIONEERS IN
BETTER TRANSPORTATION**

This advertisement commemorating the Model T Ford was prepared by Budd Body Company in 1953, the automaker's "Golden Jubilee" year. Budd was a longtime supplier of Ford automobile bodies. As the advertisement notes, the two companies traced their association all the way back to 1918, when Budd was producing parts for the Model T.

1923-1932
The Jazz Age

During the 1920s, the automobile became a symbol of youth and social change in America. Young motorists discovered that their new-found mobility translated into greater freedom and independence. The nation's puritanical character, a reflection of its British extraction, began to give way to a more informal lifestyle brought about by the auto age. Sociologists of the period noted conflicts between the new "motor car movement" and family or religious values. Cars of the era began to reflect an image of cultural self-indulgence with the first styling studios evolving and multi-colored paint jobs replacing basic black. At the high end of the spectrum, truly opulent machines with massive proportions and custom coach built bodies appeared. But, even bread-and-butter cars, like Ford's new Model A, became richer-looking. When the "Jazz Age" turned into the Great Depression, change in the automobile was inevitable. It came slowly, though. The 1932 Chevrolet still resembled a Cadillac, while Ford's 1932 offering was essentially a "baby Lincoln." The motorization of America would pause for a moment, as the economy faltered. However, it would not come to a full stop.

1923 Dagmar 6-70. *Advertised as "An Automobile Classic," the Dagmar was a large, sporty car built in Hagerstown, Maryland. Only 135 were made in 1923. The 70-horsepower Continental six was mounted in a 138-inch wheelbase. Prices were in the $3,500 to $4,500 range.*

1923 Doble Model E. *Early Dobles were built in Massachusetts and Michigan. The company moved to Emeryville, California in 1923 when the "E" was introduced. It was one of the finest steam cars ever made. The four-cylinder engine produced 75-horsepower and had a condenser that allowed 1,500 miles of driving on 24 gallons of water. The custom-bodied Dobles started at nearly $9,000; some cost over $11,000.*

1923 Chevrolet Superior. *Introduced in 1923, the Superior was a car that launched a successful Chevrolet challenge to Ford's market domination. The 135-cubic-inch overhead-valve four produced 22 horsepower. Almost 500,000 of these cars were built in 1923.*

1923 Stearns-Knight Six. *Cleveland, Ohio was the home of Stearns-Knight from 1912-1929. The company said that it built cars for "Mr. Substantial Citizen." The 63-horsepower six of 1923 sold between $2,700 and $3,700. It was a substantially-priced, prestige automobile.*

1924 Cadillac V-63. *Competing with Lincoln for sales, Cadillac vastly improved the engineering of its 314.5-cubic-inch V-8 in the fall of 1923. The result was an increase from 60 to 80 horsepower. Another new feature of the V-63 was four-wheel brakes.*

1924 Lexington "Minute Man" Six. *Built in Kentucky by a racehorse promoter, the Minute Man Six was the first car that won the Pike's Peak Hillclimb two years straight. For 1924, horsepower was increased to 72. Not bad for an under-$5,000 automobile.*

1924 Pilot. *"The Car Ahead," was the slogan of this Richmond, Indiana auto maker. However, Pilot was behind the eight ball in 1924, about to enter receivership. Nonetheless, cars like the 6-56 roadster had a lot to offer. This roadster featured a 126-inch wheelbase and a 68-horsepower six for just $1,745.*

1924 Star Station Wagon. *Advertised as "A Great Deal of Car for the Money," the Star was William C. Durant's Model T Ford fighter. The marque is most famous for offering America's first "factory" station wagon.*

1925 Chrysler B-70. *This was a continuation of the first, 1924, Chrysler which offered high performance at a moderate price. Selling for as little as $1,625, the Chrysler combined power with affordability. Its L-head six developed 68 horsepower with its high-for-the-time 4.7:1 compression ratio. A stripped 1924 Chrysler competed in the French Grand Prix at LeMans.*

1925 Packard Six. *For 1925, the Packard six was engineered to give better performance. The L-head six was bored out to 288.6 cubic inches producing 60 horsepower and a top speed of 72 miles per hour. Six-cylinder sales hit over 40,000, compared to 11,000 in 1924.*

1925 Kissel 75 Speedster. *A new straight eight engine made the 1925 Kissel exciting. These fine, fast cars were built in Hartford, Wisconsin. Sporty speedsters were Kissel's best known products. The 1925 Model 75 Speedster sold for about $2,500 and had 71-horsepower. Top speed was about 100 miles per hour.*

1925 Peerless 6-70. *At $2,335, the 70-horsepower Peerless was an impressive product in all regards. "Now there's a Peerless for every one," the company advertised. Also remaining available was the costlier, but no more powerful Peerless 8-67.*

1926 Locomobile 90. *Well-known engineer Barney Roos created this powerful and luxurious car. Its 371.5-cubic-inch L-head six developed 86 horsepower. Price tags of $5,500 to $7,500 covered eight models. Barney Roos would later gain fame for developing the Jeep.*

1926 Stutz AA. *The "Safety Stutz" of 1926 reflected a change in the company's management and direction. It was designed for maximum sophistication, rather than machismo. A free year's worth of passenger insurance was included in the price of each car. All models sold for $2,995 and employed a new 92-horsepower vertical eight of 287 cubic inches.*

1926 Wills St. Claire W-6. *After making a fortune building Fords he didn't believe in, C. Harold Wills lost it all trying to make the best car in the world. The W-6 featured an electric fuel pump and parts made of molybedenum steel. Only 2,085 cars were built in 1926.*

1926 McFarlan TV-6. *High-quality, prestige and limited-production continued to characterize the upscale McFarlan in the 1920s. The Twin-Valve Six displaced a massive 572.5 cubic inches and generated 120 horsepower at 2000 rpm. Each McFarlan had a unique custom body.*

1927 Reo Flying Cloud. *The new "Flying Cloud" had a 73-horsepower six with a smooth, seven-main-bearing crankshaft. It introduced Lockheed internal-expanding hydraulic brakes to the auto industry. Fabio Segardi designed its fresh-looking, low-slung lines. There were five models priced from $1,550 to $2,500.*

1927 Studebaker President. *With a 354-cubic-inch 75-horsepower L-head six, the first Studebaker President helped mark the South Bend, Indiana company's "Diamond Jubilee" anniversary. Offerings included cars with a choice of 120- and 127-inch wheelbases. The President line had three models priced from $1,810 for the Duplex Phaeton to $2,495 for the limousine.*

1927 Doble Steamer Series E. *Abner Doble was convicted of stock manipulation in 1924, but successfully appealed the lawsuit against him. Though his company suffered, it continued to build what many consider the best steam cars ever made. The Series E was such a high-quality vehicle that it survived from 1923 to 1931 with virtually no changes.*

1927 LaSalle V-8. *A companion car to the high-priced Cadillac, the LaSalle was most famous as the first model styled by Harley Earl's "Art & Colour Section" at GM. It was also a technically advanced automobile with a 303-cubic-inch 90-degree V-8 and a 125-inch wheelbase.*

1928 Dodge Victory Six. *The Victory Six, introduced Jan. 7, 1928, was considered the fastest and smartest vehicle in the $1,000 to $1,200 price class. It had a 208-cubic-inch L-head engine that produced 58 horsepower. A 112-inch wheelbase was featured.*

1928 Ford Model A. *Replacing the venerable Model T, the "New Ford" had Lincoln-like styling in a smaller scale. With prices starting at $460, the Model A used a capable 200.5-cubic-inch four that gave 40 horsepower. The first Model A was built on October 20, 1927.*

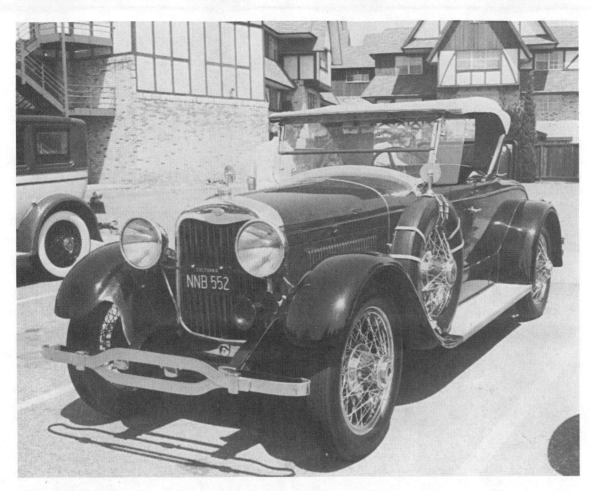

1928 Lincoln Model L. *Henry Ford had the 1928 Lincoln re-engineered to give more power. The L-head V-8 was bored out to 385 cubic inches for 81 horsepower. Also new was a counter-balanced crankshaft for greater smoothness of operation. Although big, the Lincoln had great roadability and was always a pleasure to drive down the road.*

1928 Chrysler Imperial. *The Imperial's job was to make Chrysler competitive in the prestige car market-place. A 309.3-cubic-inch L-head six powered the 1928 L-80 model. It had a high-for-the-time 6.0:1 compression ratio and 100 horsepower. Fifteen custom-bodied models on a 136-inch wheelbase were offered. A 1928 Imperial placed second in the year's Belgian Grand Prix.*

1929 DuPont Model G. *Released in 1929, the Model G was an all-new eight-cylinder car that came on 135- and 141-inch wheelbases. The 322-cubic-inch engine generated 125-horsepower and compared favorably to the previous 70-horsepower DuPont six. It was a world-class car in terms of styling, quality and performance.*

1929 DeSoto Model K. *The first car to bear the DeSoto name was destined to set an all-time industry sales record for new models released through that time. It filled a market gap between Dodges and Chryslers as an upper-medium-priced automobile. Under the hood was a 174.9-cubic-inch L-head six with 55 horsepower that gave performance to match its good looks. Prices for seven models were $845 to $955.*

1929 Duesenberg Model J. *Errett L. Cord bought Duesenberg out of receivership to make a new luxury model for Auburn Automobile Company. A classic among classics, the J entered production in December 1928. Its 420-cubic-inch straight eight was good for 208 horsepower and 116 miles per hour. The Custom-built bodies used on Duesenbergs came on 142.4- and 153.5-inch wheelbases, the chassis alone costing $8,500.*

1929 Kissel White Eagle. *The White Eagle name first appeared on 100 speedsters made in 1928. With 298-cubic-inch eight-cylinder engines, they were good for 115 horsepower and 100 miles per hour. For 1929, all Kissels, even sixes, were called White Eagles. However, the name seems always to evoke images of the 1929 speedster-eight, which offered sports car buffs 126 horsepower that season.*

1930 Cadillac V-16. *A "Great Gatsby" era land yacht of the highest order, the Cadillac V-16 was designed as the ultimate luxury car. Its 452-cubic-inch motor developed 185 horsepower. With its very limited market, the V-16 realized 3,251 sales over two model years. It could make 90 miles per hour.*

1930 Ruxton. *Entrepreneur Archie M. Andrews organized a loose network of different automakers to build cars for his New Era Motors. The front-wheel-drive Ruxton was produced by Moon in St. Louis, Missouri and Kissel in Hartford, Wisconsin. It was an elegant, sporty and handsomely styled car. About 500 were made, most by Moon, although it's reported Kissel built 25.*

1930 Cord L-29. *Inspired by Harry Miller's front-wheel-drive Indianapolis 500 race cars the L-29 Cord was conceived as E.L. Cord's "sports car" to complement his lower-priced Auburns and upscale Duesenbergs. Low-slung on a 137.5-inch wheelbase, the L-29 had a 298.6-cubic-inch Lycoming straight-eight engine.*

1930 Nash Twin-Ignition Eight. *The first Nash eight was introduced October 1, 1929. It had a 298.6-cubic-inch overhead-valve engine with dual ignition that produced 100 horsepower. Offering 124- and 136-inch wheelbases, these Nash 490s were the largest cars that the Kenosha, Wisconsin company had built up to that time.*

1931 Elcar Model 130. *Founded in 1916 by William and George Pratt, this Elkhart, Indiana marque built durable cars that were often used as taxicabs. The Model 130 featured a 140-horsepower eight and a 130-inch wheelbase. It sold for just below $2,000. Elcar was hurt by the depression and entered receivership in 1931.*

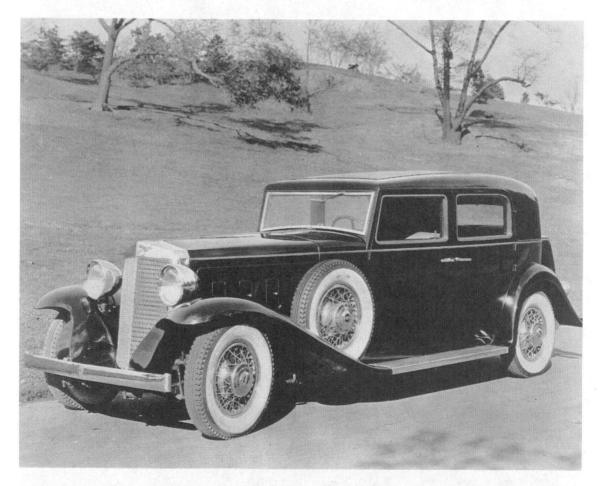

1931 Marmon 16. *A monument to the precision engineering interests of Howard Marmon, the V-16 was a super-car offering the best power-to-weight ratio of any 1931 American automobile. The 490-cubic-inch engine cranked out 200 horsepower. It could move the 6,000-pound custom-bodied Marmons to 100 miles per hour. Only 390 Marmon V-16s were made.*

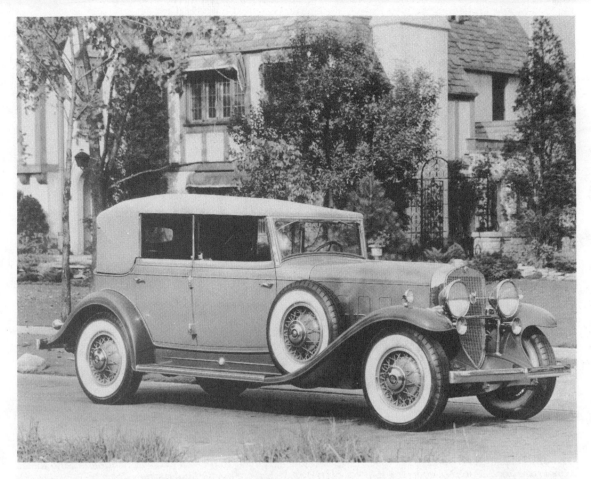

1931 Cadillac V-12. *Another reflection of Cadillac's superiority in the luxury class was the V-12 that bowed in September 1930. Specifications included a 368-cubic-inch engine, 134- or 140-inch wheelbases and a three-speed transmission. With 135 horsepower, the V-12 performed on a level with the more costly V-16.*

1931 Lincoln Model K. *The Model K moved Lincoln stylishly ahead in the luxury car field. Its flowing lines made the earlier models look stodgy. A 384.8-cubic-inch V-8 of 120 horsepower made the 145-inch wheelbase Lincolns real performers, too. The K was the first American car with a two-barrel carburetor.*

1932 Ford V-8. *Henry Ford set an automotive milestone by building a V-8 the average motorist could afford. The 221-cubic-inch 65-horsepower motor created a low-priced car that could keep up with all but the fastest cars on the road. Priced as low as $460, the early Ford V-8s were hot and handsome cars.*

1932 Packard Twin-Six. *Packard's entry in the multi-cylinder car derby was a V-12 of 445.5 cubic inches and 160 horsepower. It was offered on 142- or 147-inch wheelbase cars that carried the finest custom coach-built bodies. Top speed was conservatively advertised at 85 miles per hour. Prices ranged from $3,650 to $7,750.*

1932 Plymouth PB. *The PB didn't last long, but today it's considered the most desirable of four-cylinder Plymouths and the best. It had a "big car" look, because it was designed to accommodate a six. The 196.1-cubic-inch, 65-horsepower engine was linked to a three-speed transmission. A $40 option was a Collegiate Special roadster painted in the colors of the owner's university.*

1932 Reo Royale. *Reo's doomed luxury car debuted in the depression. Priced at a reasonable $1,985 to $2,995 for 131- and 135-inch wheelbase models, these large and classy-looking machines had a smooth-running straight eight with nine main bearings and 125 horsepower. Only 3,560 Reos of all types were built in 1932.*

The Airflow CHRYSLER
Brings a New Form of Travel

* * * * * * * * *

In one master stroke of engineering, the new Airflow* Chrysler brings to the motor car the spacious comfort of the drawing room . . . a brilliant new functional beauty . . . a new conception of strength and safety . . . and a silent floating ease of motion that surpasses any known form of travel on land or sea or air.

There is an entirely new system of weight distribution. The engine is over the front axle. The rear seat is 20 inches forward of the rear axle. The passengers ride at the center of balance . . . cradled between the two axles. The periodicity—or rate of spring action— has been greatly slowed down. The motion of the car becomes a long easy glide . . . like riding on a cushion of air.

In appearance . . . in speed . . . in efficiency . . . in roominess and riding comfort . . . the new Airflow Chrysler opens whole new horizons of motoring. When you see it and ride in it, you will know for yourself that it brings an entirely new and infinitely finer form of travel.

FLOATING RIDE BOOKLET FREE—Write for the interesting booklet which describes the romantic development of Floating Ride. Address the Chrysler Sales Corporation, 12211 East Jefferson Ave., Detroit, Mich.

Four Distinctive 1934 Models Chrysler Airflow Eight . . . 122 horsepower and 123-inch wheelbase. Six-pass. Sedan, Brougham and Town Sedan, five-pass. Coupe. All body types, $1245. Chrysler Airflow Imperial . . . 130 horsepower . . . 128-inch wheelbase. Six-pass. Sedan and Town Sedan, five-pass. Coupe. All body types, $1495. Airflow Custom Imperial . . . 150 horsepower . . . 146-inch wheelbase . . . magnificently-styled, individualized body types. 1934 Chrysler Six . . . *With independently sprung front wheels* . . . for a levelized, cushioned ride . . . 93 horsepower, 7 body types on 118-inch and 121-inch wheelbase. Priced from $725 up. Four-door Sedan, $795. *All Prices F. O. B. Factory, Detroit.*   *NAME COPYRIGHTED 1933—CHRYSLER CORPORATION

Chrysler's classic marketing blunder was introducing the Airflow during the Depression. Though featuring futuristic styling and advanced technology, the car was too far ahead of its time to succeed. This ad dates from 1934.

1933-1942
The Designer Decade

In the fifth decade of the American auto, the big change in cars was visual. Industrial design, a merger of science and art, was becoming an important force in product development. The Great Depression brought pressure to create radically different looking cars that would obsolete old ones and enhance sales of new ones. At the same time, new materials and manufacturing processes evolved that made it possible to bring designers' visions to the production line. In the early '30s, designers focused on pure aerodynamics and the torpedo or teardrop shape. However, extremely aerodynamic cars proved unpopular in the marketplace. Ultimately, it was pseudo-aerodynamic styling, marked by massive rounded forms and longer, lower, rectilinear shapes that prevailed. There were few major technological revolutions in this era other than all-steel body construction, which complemented the new styling trends. This was the first era in which engineering advances took a back seat to appearance enhancements. The result was a 10-year period that spurred many beautiful and trend-setting car designs.

1933 Pierce-Arrow Silver Arrow. *The streamlined Silver Arrow was predictive of new styling trends with its fastback roofline and slab sides. Only five of these $10,000 cars were built. A new feature found on 1933 Pierce-Arrows was an engine with hydraulic valve lifters.*

1933 Stutz DV-32. *The legendary Bearcat name was revived by Stutz to create a sports car that could do over 100 miles per hour. Its engine was a refined version of the vertical-eight with double overhead cams and four valves per cylinder. In Super Bearcat form, the 156-horsepower engine was installed in a racy speedster on a short 116-inch wheelbase chassis.*

1933 Chrysler Imperial Custom CL. *With styling reminiscent of the L-29 Cord, the Imperial was extremely handsome and technically sophisticated in a conventional way. A 385-cubic-inch L-head eight with 135 horsepower was linked to the new three-speed "silent synchromesh" transmission.*

1933 Continental. *This car has no relationship to the better-known Lincoln-Continental nameplate. It hails from Grand Rapids, Michigan and was built only in 1933 and 1934. For 1933, there were Beacon, Flyer and Ace series, while only the Beacon line returned in 1934. Only 3,310 cars were made in the first year and a mere 953 were built during 1934.*

1934 Dymaxion. *Buckminster Fuller designed this car-of-the-future as an experiment in pure aerodynamics. It had two wheels up front and one behind. Powered by a Ford V-8, it went 120 miles per hour and 40 miles on a gallon of gas. Three cars, all slightly different, were built.*

1934 Terraplane Deluxe Six. *Introduced in 1932 as a Hudson Essex, the Terraplane was a speedy, low-priced six that could do 80 miles per hour. The Essex part of the name was dropped in 1934, when the Terraplane grew larger and got a 212-cubic-inch 85-horsepower six. Flowing front and rear fenders gave the '34 a more streamlined look.*

1934 Packard 12 LeBaron Sport Phaeton. *Often considered among the handsomest Packards ever built, the LeBaron sport phaeton sold for $7,746. Its 445.5-cubic-inch V-12 developed 160 horsepower and pushed the 5,400-pound two-passenger sports-luxury car to 60 miles per hour in 20.4 seconds. The custom-built LeBaron body was a knock-out.*

1934 Duesenberg SJ. *Before he died in an auto accident, Fred Duesenberg designed a centrifugal supercharger for his Model J. The result was a boost to 320 horsepower and a top speed of 129 miles per hour for this SJ. Following industry trends, the custom bodies appearing on the $9,500 Duesenberg chassis grew increasingly modern-looking due to the influence of streamlining.*

1935 Pontiac "Silver Streak." *Pontiac was the only General Motors nameplate introduced after formation of the corporation to succeed. Early Pontiacs were very good sellers, then the depression came. The restyled 1935 models put the company back on the sales charts, almost doubling sales. Buyers liked the art deco "waterfall" grille, the all-steel turret-top and a low-priced six. The new "Silver Streak" look created by Franklin Q. Hershey gave the Pontiac a distinct identity that lasted over 20 years.*

1935 Hudson Custom 8. *Marque historians consider the '35s to be the first "modern" Hudsons. They featured the industry's first all-steel production car bodies. The L-head straight eight used in these 25th anniversary models had 254 cubic inches and 113 horsepower. British speed ace Sir Malcolm Campbell set seven speed records in a '35 Hudson at Daytona Beach, Florida. Thirty-six new stock car records were also clinched by the 1935 Hudson 8.*

1935 Chrysler Airflow. *"The beauty of nature itself," was how Chrysler introduced its Airflow in 1934. An innovative and technically superior automobile, the Airflow proved again that the car-buying public wasn't ready for pure streamlining in the '30s. Though offered in 13 models spanning the six, eight and Imperial car-lines, only 7,751 sales were realized by Chrysler Airflows in 1935.*

1935 Pierce-Arrow. *This streamlined 1935 Pierce-Arrow 12 is an extremely rare model, since only 875 Pierce-Arrows of all types were made that year. The V-12 engine produced 175 horsepower at 3400 rpm. Pierce-Arrow, founded in 1901, had only three years left when this exquisite machine was produced.*

1936 Auburn Supercharged Speedster. *Duesenberg designer Gordon Buehrig rose admirably to the task of designing an inexpensive-to-build boattail speedster body to help E.L. Cord sell his inventory of leftover Auburns. With the sporty new coach work and a supercharged straight eight engine, the slinky-looking $2,245 cars were guaranteed to do 100 miles per hour. About 500 were built.*

1936 Stout Scarab. *William B. Stout was recognized as the father of modern airplanes. His Scarab was a radically streamlined, rear-engined car using aircraft construction and many Ford parts. It had a lounge type passenger cabin and four-wheel independent suspension. About nine of the cars were built.*

1936 Buick Century. *The first Buick Century mated the company's big Roadmaster/Limited engine with a chassis only four inches longer than that of the small Buick Special. The 320-cubic-inch 120-horsepower straight eight gave the new model a speed close to the "Century mark" of 100 miles per hour. Century's sold for prices between $1,035 and $1,135 and represented a sort of "factory hot rod."*

1936 Cadillac Series 60. *A new "popular-priced" Cadillac, the Series 60 was powered by a V-8 with up-to-date engineering advances. Though small by Cadillac standards, the 322-cubic-inch motor generated 125 horsepower. In the small, Buick-sized body, the engine gave twice the gas mileage of the company's V-12 and V-16 and nearly equal performance.*

1937 Lincoln-Zephyr. *The heavily streamlined Lincoln-Zephyr featured innovative, semi-unitized body construction and a high-speed 267.3-cubic-inch V-12 with 110 horsepower. "With its advanced aerodynamics, the Zephyr could make 90 miles per hour and go 16 miles on a gallon of fuel.*

1937 Packard Super Eight. *Packard had found a degree of financial success with the low-priced 120 model it brought out in 1935. Now it needed an image car to help maintain its upscale reputation. The Super Eight was given a "just right" modern look and size for 1937. Its big 384-cubic-inch straight eight produced 150 horsepower. Priced $600 less than the Packard 12 and weighing 400 pounds less, the Super Eight was a well-balanced machine that seemed like the best of all worlds.*

1937 Cord 812 Sportsman. *Gordon M. Buehrig set long-lasting styling trends with his so-called "coffin-nose" Cord. Its advanced features included the disappearance of running boards, an alligator jaw hood and hidden headlamps. A 288.6-cubic-inch 125-horsepower V-8 powered the front-wheel drive Cord 810. For 1937, the 170-horsepower supercharged 812 version was available, too. It could hit 112 miles per hour and go 0-to-60 in 13.5 seconds.*

1937 Pierce-Arrow 12. *Pierce-Arrow was the only luxury carmaker to survive through 1937 without branching out into the mid-priced field. The company's top-of-the-line model was the 185-horsepower Pierce-Arrow 12 series with 13 models and three massive wheelbases: 139, 144 or 147 inches.*

1938 Chrysler New York Special. *The Airflow was gone, but Chrysler had a new model based on its big Imperial. The New York Special coupe and sedan had unique grilles with wider horizontal openings and special broadcloth upholstery. They were the first of what would become the Chrysler New Yorker models. Below the hood was a 248.7-cubic-inch 110-horsepower straight eight.*

1938 American Bantam Roadster. *The American Austin was an early 1930s economy compact based on the diminutive English Austin. For 1938, a similar-sized car with no direct link to Austin was built by the same Pennsylvania firm. With modernized body styling by Count Alexis de Sakhnoffsky, the American Bantam made an especially modern and handsome-looking little roadster.*

1938 Studebaker President 8. *Smoother styling and lower, wider bodies modernized the 1938 Studebaker models. Powering the seven President models was a 250.5-cubic-inch 110-horsepower inline eight. A new option was the vacuum-operated "Miracle Shift" transmission. Only 5,474 Presidents and State Presidents were built.*

1938 Cadillac Sixty Special. *A sensational restyling gave the Sixty Special four-door sedan a very clean, crisp appearance of understated elegance. The disappearance of running boards was one secret of its fresh design. The Sixty Special had its own 127-inch wheelbase and a $2,085 price tag.*

1939 Graham "Sharknose." *"Spirit of Motion" styling featured an art deco "ship's prow" nose and forward-humped fenders with squarish headlamps. It was new, it was different, it was modern, and it was unpopular with the buying public. Power came from a "supercharged" six-cylinder engine.*

1939 Hupp Skylark. *Lincoln-Zephyr creator John Tjaarda restyled the famous "coffin nose" Cord body to create the Hupp Skylark. Unlike the Cord, it was a rear-drive car on the Hupmobile 115-inch-wheelbase chassis. However, Hupp was broke and the production of the cars was handled by Graham-Paige, which also made its own Hollywood version. Production of both cars was very limited.*

1939 Mercury 8. *It could be regarded as a medium-priced big Ford or a small Lincoln. Ford preferred the latter image and gave the Mercury enough appointments and power to compete with cars like Oldsmobile, Buick and Chrysler. Designed to fill a market niche between the Ford and the Lincoln-Zephyr, the first "Merc" had a 116-inch wheelbase and a 95-horsepower flathead V-8.*

1939 Plymouth Deluxe Convertible Sedan. *Walter P. Chrysler's low-priced car bowed in 1928 and he timed the arrival of the Plymouth perfectly. It helped Chrysler survive the Great Depression. One of the most collectible models is the rare, one-year-only convertible sedan. Only 387 were built.*

1940 Ford Deluxe V-8. *Styling made the 1940 Ford one of the year's outstanding American cars. It has a "just right" appearance that's considered a classic design. It gave the Ford a richer, big car image to go with the big car performance of its flathead V-8. The "woodie" station wagon was $875.*

1940 Packard Darrin 180. *Designer Howard "Dutch" Darrin took the conservative Packard and turned it into a big, sporty high-performance machine dubbed "The Glamour Car of the Year." With cut-down doors and no running boards, the Darrin looked fast standing still, The 180 model was on the big, fast Super Eight chassis.*

1940 Chevrolet Special Deluxe. *Chevrolet's new-for-1940 "Royal Clipper" styling turned it into a low-priced car that looked expensive. A longer 113-inch wheelbase completed this new image. Even though Chevrolet lacked a straight eight or V-8, Juan Manuel Fangio won a 6,000-mile Argentina endurance race in a six-cylinder 1940 Chevrolet coupe.*

1940 Lincoln-Continental. *The idea behind the design and name of the first Lincoln-Continental was to create an American car with European-like sophistication. It looked like a custom-built car with its clean, squared-off format and no running boards. The proven Lincoln-Zephyr mechanicals were used.*

1941 Oldsmobile 98 Phaeton. *Oldsmobile made its two millionth car in 1941, but the big news from the Lansing, Michigan company was the rich, rare 98 series. The four 98 models were Oldsmobile's answer to the Cadillac. They had large dimensions and a big eight-cylinder engine. Less than 25,000 of them were made.*

1941 Pontiac Custom Torpedo 8. *Launched as a light six with fine car features that was priced slightly higher than bottom-line cars, the value-packed Pontiac became America's best-selling mid-priced automobile during 1941. The Custom Torpedo 8 was at the top-of-the-line, using GM's big C-body to provide one-step-up buyers with an affordable big car.*

1941 Chrysler Town & Country. *Chrysler was America's 10th largest automaker in 1941. Company president David D. Wallace designed the Town & Country as a luxury car for the nation's "landed gentry." The unique barrel-back body with white ash framing and mahogany panels gave the dual-purpose car/station wagon a rich, rustic appearance.*

1941 Willys-Overland Jeep. *Though far from aerodynamic or streamlined, the Jeep fits well in the "Designer Decade." It was designed to meet specific U.S. Army criteria for a rugged General Purpose (GP) vehicle that could go anywhere. Willys was the winner among several firms that competed for the lucrative contract to make the military model.*

1942 Cadillac Derham Town Car. *The one-two punch of the Great Depression and World War II knocked the custom coach-work industry for a loop; one from which it would never recover. Coach builders such as Le-Baron and Derham would find few customers after the war. The situation wasn't much better in 1942, when this rare custom was crafted. Only six Derham Town Cars were built.*

1942 Nash 600. *The 1942 Nash 600 was the company's least expensive model. It was also the perfect car to own for World War II "home-front" use, as gas and tire rationing became realities. Roomy and reliable, the "600" indicated how far it would travel on a 20-gallon tankful of fuel. And for just $940, you got the revolutionary "unitized" Nash body construction, too.*

1942 Studebaker Champion. *For Americans who had to keep going while the boys were fighting the bad guys, this was another great car to own. The 170-cubic-inch six gave 80 horsepower and a coupe was only $785. The 110-inch wheelbase made it family-sized, as well.*

1942 DeSoto. *DeSoto offered 14 models in 1942. The three-passenger business coupe for $1,028 didn't seem too far removed from the limousine at $1,405. The taxi-proven DeSoto six lasted forever, got you around town, and didn't waste ration coupons. The hidden headlamps were 30 years ahead of time on a mass-production car.*

Studebaker is building an unlimited quantity of airplane engines, military trucks and other matériel for national defense . . . and a limited number of passenger cars which are the finest Studebakers ever produced

The Studebaker Corporation

Announcing three new

STUDEBAKERS FOR 1942

The President 8 ★ The Commander ★ The Champion

ORIGINATOR of the thrilling new Skyway Styling that has been the talk of motoring America for months, Studebaker now strides still farther forward in design.

And thanks to the resourcefulness and research of Studebaker's engineering and production staffs, materials critical to national defense have been released for that purpose—without any impairment of Studebaker's traditional standards of quality.

Brand-new Studebaker models for 1942 are now on view at Studebaker showrooms all over the nation—the finest motor cars Studebaker has ever offered the public.

See your local Studebaker dealer now and go for a trial drive. You may use your present car as part payment—C. I. T. terms.

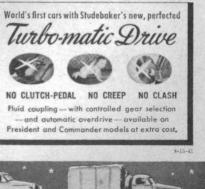

World's first cars with Studebaker's new, perfected

Turbo-matic Drive

NO CLUTCH-PEDAL   NO CREEP   NO CLASH

Fluid coupling — with controlled gear selection — and automatic overdrive — available on President and Commander models at extra cost.

Automakers contributed quite a bit to the fight for freedom in World War II. This advertisement for the 1942 President Eight shows that Studebaker was already building airplane engines and military trucks for national defense.

1943-1952
The Brave and the Bold

   While viewing American cars as "prewar" and "postwar" models is common, 1942 automobiles share a lot historically and conceptually with the bold developments of the early '50s. Many advances in design and technology were in the planning stages when the war interrupted them. Designers were dreaming of small cars, hardtops, tailfins and envelope bodies before the attack on Pearl Harbor took us into the fray. Overhead valve V-8s, practical automatic transmissions, power accessories and air conditioning were all coming into use before we went to war. After fighting began, automakers rose bravely to the challenge of helping to equip the world's greatest army. When the smoke had cleared, the bold task of shaping the future of transportation went on even as the assembly lines churned to meet postwar demand with prewar product. Then, it was 1950 and the fantasies of the '40s began rolling into showrooms to show us what the future looked like.

1943 Dodge Command Cars. *One of the most collectible types of military vehicles built by Dodge was the Command Car. This photograph shows the early 1/2-ton version on the right, with the later 1/2-ton version in the center and the 3/4-ton version at the left.*

1943 Ford GPW. *Ford Motor Company's production facilities were used to produce Jeeps for the war effort. The Ford GPW was based on the Willys-Overland design, but had some distinctions that makes it appealing to military vehicle collectors.*

1945 Studebaker. *The Studebaker factory in South Bend, Indiana did not manufacture cars during World War II, but military trucks like this one were built for the war effort.*

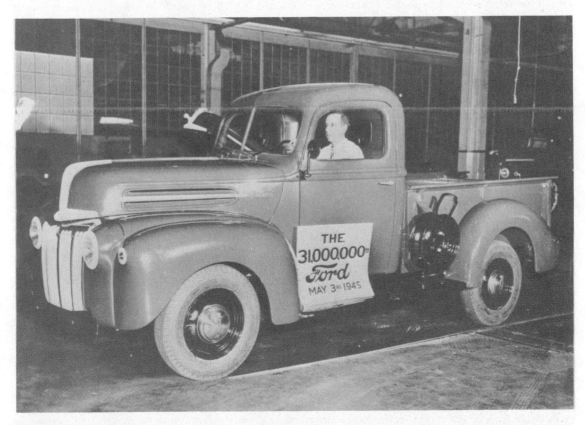

1945 Ford Pickup. *An accute shortage of light-duty trucks existed at the end of World War II. As soon as the war ended, manufacturers like Ford and Chevrolet were allowed to build "interim" models. This one rolled down the assembly line May 3, 1945 and was promoted as the 31,000,000th Ford.*

1946 Chrysler Town & Country. *When the wood-bodied Chrysler Town & Country returned after the war, the original barrel-back body was replaced with a $2,718 four-door sedan and a $2,725 convertible. It was part of the New Yorker series, with a 114-horsepower straight eight. Seven hardtops were built, but this model didn't reach regular production.*

1946 Ford Sportsman. *Ford released the Sportsman convertible at a price of $1,982. That included a specially made body of wood frame-and-panel construction. As in other Super Deluxe Fords, the 100-horsepower flathead V-8 was standard. Only 723 of the 1946 Sportsman convertibles were built.*

1946 Lincoln-Continental. *A new egg-crate grille updated the Continental's appearance after the war. The cabriolet was $4,474; the coupe was $4,392. Only 466 were made and only 201 had ragtops. They were the only 12-cylinder American postwar cars. The 305-cubic-inch V-12 produced 130 horsepower.*

1946 Willys Station Wagon. *This Brooks Stevens' design is credited with being the first all-steel station wagon. It paved the way towards making this body style affordable and practical for American families, as woody wagons were expensive and costly to maintain. The Willys wagon was based on the Army jeep, but had two-wheel-drive. It sold for $1,495 and 6,533 were made.*

1947 Cadillac Series 62 Convertible. *The 1947 Cadillac Series 62 convertible is one of the year's most collectible American cars because of its rarity. Only 1,342 of these classically-styled ragtops were manufactured. They had a list price of $2,556 and weighed 4,475-pounds. A 150-horsepower flathead V-8 was under the long, swoopy hood.*

1947 Frazer Manhattan. *"Dutch" Darrin's daring '47 Frazer won a gold medal for Design Achievement from New York's Fashion Academy. Carlton B. Spencer's color-coordinated interiors helped. Industrialist Joe Frazer gets credit for starting the Willow Run, Michigan company that made the first postwar car.*

1947 Studebaker. *Famed industrial designers Raymond Loewy and Virgil Exner teamed up to create Studebaker's first all-new postwar car. It replaced the "fat fender" look of the past with flush front end sheet metal that brought many shoppers into Studebaker showrooms.*

1947 Crosley. *Cincinnati's Powel Crosley made a small fortune selling appliances, then brought out a small car. This was a predecessor of today's "commuter car" made for short hops to the grocery store. Early versions had a copper-brazed (COBRA) engine, which was not one of Crosley's strong points.*

1948 Tucker Torpedo. *Preston Tucker was an over-optimistic inventor who tried to give America a high-tech dream car at a low price. Farsighted engineer Alex Tremulis helped create only 51 of the streamliners, which were doomed to failure in an industry dominated by compromise. The Tucker's disc brakes, seat belts, padded dash and rear-mounted helicopter engine put a scare into the complacent Big Three, who helped "torpedo" the Tucker Torpedo.*

1948 Packard Super Eight Victoria Convertible. *The Twenty-Second Series Packards were introduced in 1948. New features included a longer hood, an "ox-yoke" grille and smoother, more rounded body lines. A 145-horsepower straight eight was used. The ragtop sold for $3,250 and production for 1948 was 4,750.*

1948 Hudson "Step-Down." *With a sleek envelope body sitting low inside its frame rails, the new '48 Hudson was sure-footed and aerodynamically superior to its contemporaries. Designer Frank Spring headed the styling of the unit-bodied Hudson, which became a champion in early stock car races.*

1948 Willys Jeepster. *This Brooks Stevens design concept was so good that it came back to life in the '70s. This was America's first genuine sports utility vehicle, despite the fact that the classic 1948-1951 models did not incorporate four-wheel drive like the Jeep that sired them.*

1949 "Shoe Box" Ford. *This slab-sided all-new postwar car took its maker out of the old-fashioned "Henry Ford" era. Gone were the antiquated transverse springs and torque-tube driveshaft of previous models. Henry Ford had passed away in 1947. Now, his company was passing into the future with a modern automobile.*

1949 Buick Riviera. *When unveiled in mid-1949, the new Buick hardtop pointed the direction that American car designers were heading in. It combined the sporty lines of a convertible with the comfort and convenience of a closed car and started a styling revolution that lasted a quarter of a century. Leather and cloth upholstery and power windows were standard.*

1949 Cadillac Coupe deVille. *In addition to its futuristic hardtop styling, the Cadillac Coupe deVille came with a 331-cubic-inch overhead-valve V-8 that developed 160 horsepower. These features, plus its stylish tail-fins, gave car buyers a peek into the '50s. The 1949 Coupe deVille cost $3,496 and 8,000 were made.*

1949 Oldsmobile Rocket 88. *The big-engined, small-bodied Rocket 88 was king of the road and racetrack in 1949. It could do 0-to-60 in 12 seconds and travel a quarter mile in 20 seconds! A specially decorated ragtop version was the 1949 Indy Pace Car.*

1950 Mercury Monterey. *Mercury didn't have a hardtop, so it created the 1950 Monterey to fill the same market niche. A padded canvas or vinyl top and leather interior set it apart from the ordinary. At $2,146 it was quite a bargain. At the 1950 Indy 500, a Mercury was selected as Official Pace Car.*

1950 Nash Rambler. *Reviving a Nash-related name dating to 1902, the '50 Rambler was America's first luxury compact. It came with a radio, wheel discs, electric clock and custom steering wheel as standard equipment. A sedan and wagon joined the initial Convertible Landau model quickly. Rambler owners got 25-30 mpg and their own rock n' roll song about the "Little Nash Rambler" that beep-beeped a Cadillac while passing the big car in second gear.*

1950 Plymouth P-19. *An unsung milestone in American car history was a Plymouth that was really the first mid-sized postwar car. With a short 110-inch wheelbase and room for six in sedans and wagons, the P-19 was a near perfect package for everyday driving.*

1950 Studebaker "Bullet-Nose." *One of the most memorable early postwar cars was the "bullet-nose" Studebaker. Its aircraft-inspired appearance clearly pointed the direction in which auto designers were flying with their ideas. This was a car that turned heads with its bold individuality. It looked like a jet with wheels.*

1951 Kaiser Deluxe. *A total restyling of the 1951 Kaiser resulted in a car with lower, more rounded lines and increased airiness. Howard "Dutch" Darrin put a little dip in the windshield to make it distinctive looking, too. The Kaiser had a sporty image and a flare for up-to-date fashion inside and out. With color-coordinated Dragon interior options, it was dressed to kill the competition.*

1951 Chrysler New Yorker. *This car had Chrysler's first V-8 and what an engine it was. The 331.1 cubic-inch Hemi Firepower motor produced 180 horsepower at 4,000 rpm and boasted 7.5:1 compression. The powerful New Yorkers ran in the Mexican Road Races and served as the 1951 Indy 500 Pace Car. They put the horsepower race into high gear.*

1951 Henry J/Allstate. *Another "Dutch" Darrin design, the Henry J was Kaiser's attempt to save its sliding fortunes with a small, well-equipped car aimed at the basic transportation market. It came with four- or six-cylinder engines. The Allstate was a Henry J with a special plaid interior made of coated paper strands. It was sold by Sears, Roebuck & Company. The Henry J was picked "Fashion Car of the Year" by New York's Fashion Academy.*

1951 Lincoln Cosmopolitan Capri Coupe. *The Cosmopolitan was cleaned up of excess trim in 1951. The "Cosmo" Capri was a special model with canvas or vinyl padded top and a luxurious interior. The padded top predicted the coming of the popular vinyl roof in the '60s. With its handsome interior and exterior touches, the Capri helped Lincoln set an all-time sales record.*

1952 Skorpian. *We picked the Skorpian for our "American Dream Car" collection because it was a pioneer in the kit car field and an early fiberglass-bodied vehicle. Originally designed for Crosley running gear, it was built by Viking Craft Manufacturing Company of Anaheim, California.*

1952 Muntz Jet. *When television manufacturer Earl "Madman" Muntz bought race car builder Frank Kurtis' business, he modified the Kurtis-Kraft sports car to be three inches longer and turned it into America's first sports/personal car. Big Lincoln or Cadillac V-8s gave the aluminum-bodied Muntz a top speed of 108 miles per hour.*

1952 Aero Willys. MOTOR TREND gave the Aero Willys second place honors in its 1952 Engineering Achievement Awards. Not bad for a compact on a 108-inch wheelbase that was only 15 feet long. Small, but well equipped, the Aero Willys featured advanced unit-body construction and a choice of four- or six-cylinder engines. Nearly 50,000 examples were sold the first year.

1952 Hudson Hornet. A six-cylinder engine didn't keep the Hudson Hornet from whipping the V-8s in stock car races. During 1952, Hudsons won 27 of 34 NASCAR stock car races, plus 14 AAA checkered flags. The company's "Big 6" had 308-cubic-inches and special Twin-H dual carburetion for 145-horsepower. The wind-cheating fastback body was aerodynamically suited for maximum performance.

Chevrolet's striking Bel Air 2-door sedan. With 3 great new series, Chevrolet offers the widest choice of models in its field.

Why Chevrolet's eye-catching good looks
wear so well and last so long . . .

Why is it that Chevrolet stands out so distinctively among other cars? Well, take a look at the one in the picture for a minute, if you will.

Look at the smooth, gracefully rounded lines. Look at the clean, uncluttered design. Look at the slim and sweeping panel on the rear fender—an individual styling touch of the Chevrolet Bel Air models that you'll see on no other car.

All Chevrolets offer you lasting good looks. And Chevrolet alone in its field brings you the solid quality of Body by Fisher.

You'll find many other Chevrolet features that are equally fine. For example, there's Chevrolet's thrifty, high-compression power. There's the new Powerglide automatic transmission.* And there's Chevrolet Power Steering* for the last word in driving ease.

Now's a good time to look at Chevrolet— the lowest priced line in the low-price field. See your Chevrolet dealer. . . . Chevrolet Division of General Motors, Detroit 2, Michigan.

Optional at extra cost. Combination of 115-h.p. "Blue-Flame" engine and Powerglide available on "Two-Ten" and Bel Air models only. Power Steering available on all models.

MORE PEOPLE BUY CHEVROLETS THAN ANY OTHER CAR!

Following the Allied victory in World War II there was a swelling of patriotic feelings in America, as reflected by the background seen in this 1953 advertisement for America's number one selling car. Within a year, Chevrolet would be in a hot battle with Ford to maintain its title.

1953-1962
The Decade of Dazzle

American cars of the 1953-1962 era have great gobs of personality. They're colorful, flamboyant and even ostentatious. Some push good taste to the limit, but they do it with character. Most came with the stamp of a particular designer in every contour and curve. The concept of the corporate car, shaped by computer or by committee, hadn't arrived yet. So, no one confused a Chrysler with a Chevrolet or either one with a Ford. From a technical standpoint, the "advances" of the era were actually refinements of old ideas like automatic transmission, power accessories, air conditioning and supercharging. They were improved and made more readily available, but it was the designs and the designers that brought real change during these years. It was the "Designer Decade."

1953 Corvette. *Based on Chevrolet's EX-122 show car, the first Corvette was a dream machine turned into a reality. Designed by Harley Earl, it represented an American rendition of the sports car GIs had fallen in love with during World War II. It had a car-of-the-future look, automatic transmission and a special six-cylinder engine with three carburetors.*

1953 Buick Skylark. *Designer Ned Nickles did a factory version of a California custom car as a limited-edition model for Buick's 50th birthday. The Skylark "Anniversary Convertible" featured low-slung lines, a big V-8 and wire wheels. Only 1,690 were built on a one-to-a-dealer basis. The price was a cool $5,000.*

1953 Studebaker Starliner. One of designer Raymond Loewy's crowning achievements was the Starliner coupe, a clean, sporty car with timeless good looks. It had a single-piece, wraparound rear window and classic proportions. The design was recognized by the Museum of Modern Art as a postwar masterpiece.

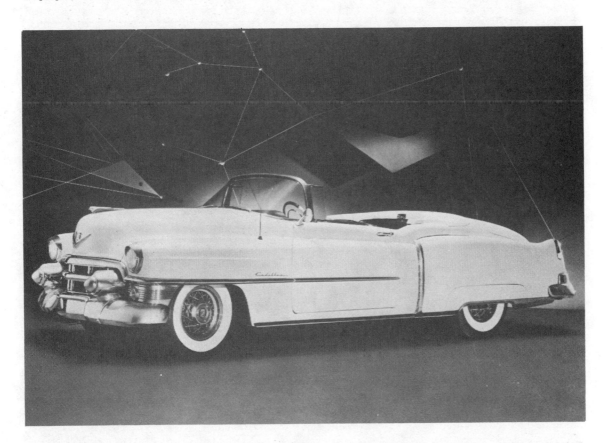

1953 Cadillac Eldorado. GM styling chief Harley Earl created a limited-edition luxury convertible to celebrate Cadillac's 50th year of automaking. It featured a profile that belonged more to a sports car than an elegant ragtop. Available only with a vast array of options for $7,750, just 532 copies were made.

1954 Kaiser-Darrin. *Howard "Dutch" Darrin gave this Kaiser sports car many unique personality traits, including a fiberglass body and doors that slid into the front fenders. Clean, rounded lines with crisp sculpturing and a small, rounded grille imparted a custom car look. At $3,655, buyers proved hard to find. Only 435 Darrins were sold.*

1954 Dodge Pace Car. *Going into the '50s, Dodge had a conservative image. However, 701 bright yellow Indy 500 Pace Cars built in 1954 changed that. Based on the upscale Royal 500 convertible, the Pace Cars included real wire wheels, a continental spare tire, a four-barrel V-8, dual exhausts, special graphics and crossed flags badges.*

1954 Hudson Italia. *Hudson's Frank Spring had his last big fling styling this European-like GT coupe for the Hudson Jet chassis. Only 27 were hand built by Carrozzeria Touring of Milan, Italy. The aluminum body had a wraparound windshield, functional air scoops and a leather interior. The Italias sold for $4,800.*

1954 Oldsmobile Starfire. *The 1954 Oldsmobile lineup included the new Starfire, a luxury convertible. With a name taken from a 1953 Motorama show car, this top-of-the-line model had special exterior moldings, leather-faced seats and a big V-8. Starfire "spinner" hubcaps became a favorite of customizers.*

1955 Ford Thunderbird. *Aimed at enthusiasts with a Walter Mitty complex and an interest in sports cars, the T-bird looked like a scaled-down Ford built for two. It came only with a V-8 and offered many amenities, including a removable hardtop made of fiberglass. With a $2,944 base price, the T-bird earned 16,155 deliveries.*

1955 Chevrolet Nomad. *The first Nomad was a station wagon version of the EX-122 Motorama dream car that sired the Corvette. When standard Chevrolets were completely restyled for 1955, a wagon with the lines of a two-door hardtop appeared. It had special styling, luxury appointments and Nomad nameplates.*

1955 Chrysler C-300. *Even with designer Virgil Exner's new "Million Dollar Look," Chrysler was having a time of it keeping up with Corvettes and T-birds in 1955. This prompted engineer Bob Rodger to create a Hemi-powered high-performance luxury car called simply the 300. With 300 horsepower, it was one of the hottest brutes on the highway. Some say it was the first muscle car.*

1955 Packard Caribbean. *Richard Teague and John Z. DeLorean were two men who shaped the "Packard Personality" in the 1950s. The Caribbean was loaded with it. Under the hood of the $6,000 specialty ragtop was Packard's first V-8. It had 352 cubic inches, 275 horsepower, and twin four-barrel carbs. Three-tone paint schemes in satin sheen lacquer highlighted the sleek body. Ultramatic transmission was standard.*

1956 Lincoln-Continental Mark II. *The Continental Mark II was a rich man's Thunderbird with classic lines and a $9,517 price. It had an ultra-clean body with long hood/short deck proportions and a formal looking roofline. The deck lid had a continental tire embossment. Powering the elegant, but sporty car was a 368-cubic-inch 285-horsepower V-8. Each Mark II was shipped in a flannel lined bag.*

1956 Dodge D-500. *A high-performance, Hemi-powered car was the D-500. It seemed like a bargain basement Chrysler 300. The 315-cubic-inch engine came with 9.25:1 compression, dual four-barrel carbs and 260 horsepower. One D-500 was driven 31,224 miles in 14 days at Bonneville, setting 306 speed records. Others like this one took 11 checkered flags in NASCAR racing.*

1956 Plymouth Fury. *Like other "family" car makers, Plymouth needed a dose of excitement to survive in the growing youth market of the '50s. The Fury combined special appearance features with a hot V-8 to get enthusiasts' hearts beating. Available only as a white hardtop with gold anodized trim, the Fury had a 240-horsepower V-8 that was good for 0-to-60 miles per hour in 9.6 seconds and 17 second quarter-mile runs.*

1956 Nash Rambler Cross Country. *Station wagons were selling like hot cakes as war-weary Americans took to the highways to forget their cares. Nash introduced the first four-door hardtop wagon in its Rambler Custom line. This Cross Country model sold for $2,326. It was available with genuine leather seat trim.*

1957 Cadillac Eldorado Biarritz. *Playing off the high interest in cars of the future, Cadillac adopted the practice of bringing out expensive specialty models that previewed the next year's styling changes. The Biarritz ragtop had distinctive trim and a unique "shark fin" rear end. It was trimmed in the richest materials and came with many accessories. Only 1,800 of these $7,286 cars were made.*

1957 Corvette "Fuelie." *Since its 1953 debut, the Corvette seemed to lack real sports car performance. This changed in 1957, when an optional fuel-injected V-8 was released. "For the first time in automotive history, one-horsepower for every cubic-inch," proclaimed ads for the car. Though only 1,040 of the 283-horsepower Vettes were made, their reputation helped keep the marque alive.*

1957 Chevrolet Bel Air Convertible. *The '57 Chevy convertible is an American cult car. This body type came only in top-of-the-line Bel Air trim. Its Cadillac-inspired styling was a big hit. Chevy's hot-to-trot small-block V-8 options gave the average car "nut" a chance to drive fast without spending money at record speed.*

1957 Ford Skyliner Retractable. *This car represented the dream of every buyer who wanted a split personality car. It could be a hardtop or a convertible at the touch of a button. The top mechanism was costly, heavy and complex, but still lots of fun. The lack of trunk storage space kept sales to 20,766.*

1958 Chevrolet Impala. *The '58 Chevrolet was totally modernized inside and outside and looked like a custom car. A new Impala series was added with a coupe and convertible. The Impala name was a hit and later became known as "the preeminent American car."*

1958 Pontiac Bonneville. *Pontiac moved its plushest car to its small chassis to create a unique model that was faster and fancier. The new Bonneville series had a sports coupe and convertible and standard 255-horsepower four-barrel V-8. Tri-Power (300 horsepower) and fuel-injected (310 horsepower) engines were optional. A Bonnevile was the Indy Pace Car.*

1958 Ford Thunderbird. *The four-passenger "square bird" converted Ford's priciest model from a sports car to a personal luxury car. It grew in size by 18 inches and in weight by 1,000 pounds. Bucket seats and a 352-cubic-inch 300-horsepower V-8 were standard. Sales sailed to 38,000, making the T-bird one of two U.S. cars to find more buyers in 1958 than 1957.*

1958 Edsel. *"The newest thing on wheels," was a Ford product for the market niche between Mercury and Lincoln. With a horse collar grille and "Tele-Touch" push-button automatic transmission, the Edsel was a high-style, high-tech auto. Buyer appeal was low, though. The 63,110 built in 1958 earned a 1.5 percent share of the market.*

1959 Cadillac. *Designed by Chuck Jordan, with inspiration from Flash Gordon, the '59 Cadillac is said to characterize the flamboyance of the '50s better than any other car. Front and rear grilles, towering fins and rocket-shaped taillights gave the "1959 Ca-doo" a decadent demeanor. A cult of collectors consider it the ultimate postwar land yacht.*

1959 Studebaker Lark. *When a recession in 1957 sent U.S. automakers racing to develop compact cars, the Lark came in first. It was basically a '58 Studebaker with dramatically shortened front and rear sections. Boxy, but roomy and reliable, the Lark helped spark a sales revival to over 100,000 cars and put black ink in the books.*

1959 Chrysler 300E. *Chrysler's 1959 "Letter Car" was most changed under the hood. The Hemi was swapped for a new wedge-head "Golden Lion" V-8 with 413 cubic inches and 380 horsepower. Though smoother idling, it kept up the 300's high-performance habits. Swivelling front seats were optional. Only 550 hardtops and 140 convertibles were built.*

1959 Pontiac "Wide-Tracks." *The first of the "Wide-Track" Pontiacs had clean lines and a split grille that sent sales soaring. Moving the wheels further apart was hailed as a major engineering advance that enhanced handling. A bigger advantage in the showroom was that it made the car look lower and wider. MOTOR TREND picked the 1959 Pontiac as its "Car of the Year."*

1960 Corvair. *With an air-cooled "pancake six" engine in the rear, all-independent suspension and a totally new-sized body, the 1960 Corvair became known as "the most significant car of the postwar era." It was radically different from anything offered by domestic automakers and gave GM another MOTOR TREND "Car of the Year" award.*

1960 Ford Falcon. *While Chevrolet's compact took awards, Ford's little car won the sales race with 435,000 deliveries. It was a simple pint-sized package that provided reliable transportation to budget-minded buyers. The development of a small Ford can be traced back to the Cardinal project started during World War II.*

1960 Mercury Comet. *Compacts from Chevrolet, Ford and Chrysler made news in 1960, but a small Mercury was bigger news yet. It was the first luxury compact, as well as the first six-cylinder Mercury. Over 125,000 were sold. The Comet was actually conceived as a successor to the Edsel.*

1960 Checker Superba. *Checker had been building "bullet-proof" taxis since 1923 and decided to sell to the private car buyer in 1960. The Kalamazoo, Michigan company turned out 1,050 vehicles that year, all powered by an 80-horsepower flathead six that went many miles without fuss. Today, the sight of a Checker on the street turns heads.*

1961 Impala SS. *The first of the superlative Super Sports was an Impala with a dealer kit of options installed. Included in the $54 package were emblems, spinner wheelcovers, power brakes, metallic brake linings, a tachometer and special narrow whitewalls. Only 142 Super Sports were sold in 1961, making them rare and valuable.*

1961 Lincoln-Continental. *As in 1941 and 1956, Lincoln turned out a classic Continental for 1961. It showed how strikingly beautiful a production automobile could be. The clean, slab-sided lines looked elegant and sophisticated. An exciting new model was a four-door convertible that found just 2,857 buyers.*

1961 Dodge Lancer. *The Dodge Lancer was a handsome rendition of the Valiant compact that Chrysler-Plymouth Division launched in 1960. It had similar Virgil Exner styling and a custom-car-like horizontal bar grille. Sales of 74,773 Lancers showed a strong market for this type of Dodge and set the stage for the coming of the Dart.*

1961 Ford Thunderbird. *The 1961 Thunderbirds were entirely new. Longer, lower and wider, they came as a hardtop coupe or convertible. The first cost $4,170 and had a production run of 62,535. The ragtop was $4,637 and 10,516 were made. One 1961 Thunderbird convertible served as the Indy 500 Pace Car.*

1962 Pontiac Grand Prix. *A lot of people don't realize the Grand Prix bowed in 1962, taking the place of the Ventura-trimmed Catalina at the last moment. It was aimed at the sports/personal car market. Bucket seats and a tachometer were standard equipment in the $3,490 Sport Coupe. Sales hit 30,195.*

1962 Studebaker GT Hawk. *A new Gran Turismo Hawk had a squared roofline, no tailfins and bright rocker panel moldings. It sported a Brooks Stevens' redesign that made a 10-year-old body seem fresh and up-to-date. Bucket seats and a V-8 were standard. Only 9,335 were made.*

1962 Buick Special V-6. *"A V-6 that gives you the smooth, V-lively Voom of big cars, plus gas economy that challenges the compacts" was what Buick promised in advertisements for its 1962 Special convertible, sedan or wagon models. It was the first V-6 offered in an American production car and earned MOTOR TREND "Car of the Year" honors.*

1962 Chevy II. *Designed to steal away some of the Falcon's appeal, the Chevy II was very similar in concept to the small Ford with boxy styling and simple mechanicals. It came in 100, 300 and Nova 400 series, the last including the sporty hardtop and convertible models. A four-cylinder engine was available in all lines, except the Nova 400, which had a six as standard equipment. Over 325,000 were built.*

THERE'S SOMETHING EXTRA ABOUT OWNING AN OLDSMOBILE!

THE CAR THAT SPELLS "LUXURY" WITH CAPITAL LETTERS

A magnificent new automobile makes its debut for 1963 — the Ninety-Eight LS.*
Superbly crafted . . . lavishly appointed . . . it takes its place with
the most luxurious automobiles on the road today!   *Luxury Sedan

Ninety-Eight → OLDSMOBILE
OLDSMOBILE DIVISION • GENERAL MOTORS CORPORATION

After a flirtation with compact economy cars at the end of the 1950s, American car buyers swung back to full-sized luxury cars in the prosperous early 1960s era. A limited-edition 1963 Oldsmobile model was the Ninety-Eight LS. The initials, according to this advertisement, stood for Luxury Sedan

1963-1972
Wild in the Streets

America went wild in the streets during its eighth decade of automobiles. The '50s had taught Detroit that racing sold cars. In the '60s, it decided to build race cars for the street. They were machines with more brute force than anyone needed to fetch milk and eggs from the market. Shiny, noisy, Coke bottle-shaped cars with subtle chrome highlights and fat tires mounted on spoked wheels. They looked mean, menacing and macho. Fender badges, hood scoops and body stripes advertised their wild intention to melt the pavement and set the streets on fire.

1963 Corvette "Split Window." *The first Corvette coupe was a beauty, Chevrolet couldn't build them fast enough. Buyers had to wait up to two months to get one. Power options ranged up to a 375-horsepower fuel-injected V-8. The name for the model was inspired by the stingrays designer Bill Mitchell saw during a Florida fishing trip. Only 10,594 were ever built.*

1963 Buick Riviera. *Originally planned as a Cadillac, the Riviera brought new class and elegance to Buick's model lineup. Designer Bill Mitchell viewed it as part Rolls-Royce and part Jaguar. Buick held production of the 1963 model to 40,000 units to make the car more appealing to buyers. At least 10,000 more could have been sold.*

1963 Studebaker Avanti. *Studebaker considered reviving the Packard name for the Avanti. The fiberglass-bodied personal/luxury car, which went into production in record time, was a dramatic attempt to revitalize sagging sales. Raymond Loewy designed the car. With the supercharged R-2 V-8, it generated 289 horsepower from 289 cubic inches.*

1963 Ford Galaxie "Fastback." *At the 1963 Riverside 500 stock car race, Ford introduced a new "Total Performance" Galaxie with a wind-cheating fastback roofline. It was called the Sportsroof model. With a 427-cubic-inch competition engine, the sleek-looking car could hit 160 miles per hour on the superspeedways.*

1964 Pontiac GTO. *Pontiac's sales-generating drag racing program was threatened by a 1963 GM ban on corporate racing activity. John Z. Delorean and Jim Wangers had to sneak the GTO on the market as a LeMans option. Distinctive trim, sporty equipment and a special high-performance engine were in the $295 package. The hottest GTO could cover the quarter mile in less than 15 seconds.*

1964-1/2 Mustang. *When Ford announced the "birth of a new breed of car" at the 1964 New York World's Fair, it had no idea that the Mustang would become the best-selling new car in history. This "pony car" had the appeal of a two-seat T-bird with four-passenger seating, plus an options list that covered many market segments and widened its salability. The base model was $2,600.*

1964 Plymouth Barracuda. *This was America's first sports compact car, beating the Mustang to the show-rooms by several weeks. Its most distinctive feature was a fastback-style big rear window. Front bucket seats and a 170-horsepower six were standard, but a popular option was Chrysler's 273-cubic-inch small-block V-8 with 180 horsepower.*

1964 Cadillac. *America's top luxury car builder didn't offer a muscle car, though a powerful 429-cubic-inch 340-horsepower V-8 was standard equipment. A significant new feature of the 1964 models was a Comfort Control heating and air conditioning system that set new convenience standards for the entire auto industry.*

1965 Corvair. *A new venturi-shaped body gave the Corvair a European sports car image in 1965. It came in 500, Monza and Corsa series. Corvair buyers with high-performance in mind could order the Corsa with a 180-horsepower turbocharged engine that was good for 0-to-60 miles per hour in 11 seconds and a top speed of 113 miles per hour.*

1965 Excalibur. *The first production Excalibur was designed by Brooks Stevens. Its styling and performance reflected his personal interest in classic cars and vintage racing. With an appearance based on the 1928 Mercedes, the Excalibur was originally linked to Studebaker. When that company closed, Stevens built and sold the car himself.*

1965 Shelby 427. *Race car driver Carroll Shelby put Ford V-8s in the British AC Ace body to make a muscular sports car for the streets. Weighing just over 2,000 pounds, the Cobra with the big-block 427-cubic-inch 425-horsepower engine could do 162 miles per hour.*

1965 Plymouth Sport Fury. *The Sport Fury line was the most expensive for Plymouth buyers to choose from in 1965. Bucket seats, a center console, special wheelcovers and fender skirts were standard on the $3,164 convertible. Such a car paced the Indy 500 and Plymouth released an unusual Pace Car drivetrain-only package that was optional in any Fury model.*

1966 Dodge Charger. *Fastback roofs became a sensation in the mid-'60s. The Charger was a streamlined Dodge Coronet with an "electric shaver" grille and hidden headlights. Rich, sporty looks inside and out and lots of glass gave it an airy, light-on-its-feet appearance, despite impressively large proportions.*

1966 Oldsmobile Toronado. *Envisioned as a modern LaSalle, the Toronado was a radically-styled big car with a huge 425-cubic-inch V-8 and front-wheel drive. There was truly a hint of the great classics of the '30s in its streamlined appearance. Base priced at $4,617, the first "Toro" realized 40,963 sales.*

1966 Chevelle SS-396. *The torpedo-shaped SS-396 was pure muscle car. This model came only with the 396-cubic-inch Turbo-Jet V-8 and was the only Chevelle the big-block engine was offered in. Sales raced to 72,272. The price of the coupe was $2,776. That included special features and 325 horsepower.*

1966 Ford Galaxie 7-Liter. *This top-of-the-line Ford had special wheelcovers, trim and paint stripes, as well as power disc brakes. A 428-cubic-inch, 345-horsepower V-8 was standard. Options included the same engine with 425 horsepower or the race-proven 427-cubic-inch Ford V-8 in 360 horsepower and 410 horsepower versions. A four-speed transmission was an option.*

1967 Chevrolet Camaro. *Many people considered the original Camaro a direct descendant of the Corvette. Computers were reportedly used to shape its wind-compliant body contours. Nearly 75 percent of the cars had V-8s, though a six was standard. The big-block 396 cubic-inch engine and a Z28 option package were added at midyear.*

1967 Cadillac Eldorado. *Cadillac had been working on a front-wheel-drive car for eight years. The '67 Eldorado was worth the wait. Its razor-edge styling made it look racy, but regal. A 429-cubic-inch 340-horsepower V-8 was made to go fast, but not to sip gas. Fuel economy was 10-14 miles per gallon. Sales of the $6,277 coupe came to 17,930.*

1967 Mercury Cougar. *The Cougar was Mercury's "Top Cat" version of the Ford Mustang. It had a dressier appearance and $150 higher basic price. An XR-7 edition with aircraft-type overhead console was $230 extra. A long list of other options included a television.*

1967 Plymouth Barracuda. *Contemporary car magazines said the '67 Barracuda looked like a "baby Riviera." A convertible was offered for the first time. Also new was a Formula S package of equipment suited for sports car rallies.*

1968 AMX. American Motors developed this two-seat sports coupe to change its conservative image. The AMX was a shortened Javelin with underhood muscle-power options up to 315 horsepower. Race car driver Craig Breedlove set 106 new speed records with an AMX in February 1968.

1968 Corvette Stingray. ROAD & TRACK described the curvaceous 1968 Corvette Stingray as a car that could take you on a trip without going anywhere. Engines included a pair of 327-cubic-inch V-8s and three big-block 427-cubic-inch V-8s. The hottest had three two-barrel carburetors and 435 horsepower. "All different all over," was the sales theme.

1968 Hurst/Olds. *This was the first of a series of hot Hurst/Olds models. Oldsmobile built the basic vehicle and Hurst made it look and perform like a super-car. Among several engine options was one with 360 horsepower. Silver and black finish, body stripes and H/O badges identified one of America's best built muscle cars.*

1968 Plymouth Road Runner. *The idea behind the Road Runner was to offer younger buyers a low-priced muscle car with plain trim and upholstery, but plenty of real performance hardware. The famous Road Runner cartoon character was seen on the front fenders and a special horn chirped "beep, beep" like the bird on television.*

1969-1/2 Pontiac Trans Am. *This car was originally designed as a sports racer for the small-block Trans-American race series. The production version got a big-block engine and became a midyear Firebird option. White paint and blue stripes were used on all 687 built, including just eight rare ragtops.*

1969 Lincoln-Continental Mark III. *Lincoln worked for 3-1/2 years to develop another great classic Continental. It came out in the spring of 1968 as a 1969 model. A 460 cubic-inch, 365-horsepower V-8 was below the long, wide hood. Base-priced at $6,741, the Mark III generated 30,858 sales in its first year.*

1969 Pontiac Grand Prix. CAR LIFE magazine called it a "stretched GTO" and named the GP the best-engineered car of the year. Pontiac claimed its hood was the longest ever seen on a U.S. production car. The driver's compartment looked like an airplane cockpit. Sales of the $3,866 personal/luxury car hit 112,486.

1969 Chevrolet Camaro. The specially-trimmed Indy Pace Car version RS/SS Camaro is probably the most collectible model of this marque and this era. About 100 were built for the race and 3,674 replicas were sold. The Z-11 Pace Car package cost $37, but other costly options were mandatory on Pace Cars.

1970 Chrysler Hurst 300. *George Hurst was like the "King Midas" of motor-heads; all that he touched became gold-trimmed muscle! Based on the 124-inch wheelbase Chrysler 300, this Hurst-modified special edition had a 440-cubic-inch 375-horsepower big-block V-8 that could push it to 60 miles per hour in seven-seconds. Only 501 were built and the "01" was a convertible.*

1970 Chevrolet Monte Carlo. *With stand-out new styling, the 1970 model introduced the Monte Carlo as a sporty personal/luxury coupe. With optional 454-cubic-inch engines it was a performer, too. The SS version could do 0-to-60 miles per hour in less than eight seconds. Of the 145,975 Monte Carlos made, only 3,823 were SS models.*

1970 Dodge Challenger. *Dodge was last to field a pony car with the Challenger. It was worth waiting for. The most collectible versions are the T/A or the R/T editions optioned with the "Street Hemi" engine. Dodge only made about 1,000 Challenger T/As in 1970 and just 356 Hemi Challengers were built.*

1970 Ford Maverick. *Ford introduced the Maverick near the end of the muscle car era. It was a significant car because it gave an accurate forecast of where the industry was heading. Within a few years, sporty and economical compacts in the mold of the Maverick would be in high demand everywhere.*

1971 Buick Riviera. *With a shape as sensational as the original Corvette Sting Ray coupe, the boattail Riviera had Bill Mitchell's styling genius stamped all over it. When ordered with a GS performance package, the Riviera included a 455-cubic-inch 350-horsepower V-8.*

1971 Cadillac Eldorado. *A second-generation front-wheel drive Eldorado debuted in 1971. The look was larger, rounder and more stylized. Fender skirts hid the rear wheels. The design had more in common with the original 1953 Eldorado, than with the competition-bred look of the '67.*

1971 AMC Javelin. *A sexier, sportier Javelin bowed in 1971. Its undulating fender curves, twin canopy roof and air spoiler rear window made it more Corvette-like. The first four-passenger AMX became a Javelin option package. It came with a base 360-cubic-inch 245-horsepower V-8. A 401-cubic-inch engine with 330 horsepower was $137 extra.*

1971 Dodge Charger Super Bee. *1971 was the last year that the legendary "Street Hemi" engine was offered to the public. Only 85 Dodge Hemi Chargers were produced. The monster motor generated 425 horsepower from 426 cubic inches. It was a $707 option in Charger R/Ts and an $837 option in Charger Super Bees.*

1972 Ford Gran Torino. *A more pronounced "Coke bottle" shape and Cobra-style grille created a car that writer Tom McCahill described as a "land-locked tuna sucking air." Ford's big 429-cubic-inch V-8 was among many available options. Also on the list were some wild fade-away striping packages.*

1972 Plymouth 'Cuda 340. *The 1972 'Cuda 340 signified the model's last gasp in the high-performance realm. Gone were the Barracuda convertible and the Hemi engine. 'Cuda features included a twin-scoop hood, body stripes and black-out paint schemes. The optional 340-cubic-inch small-block V-8 came with a four-barrel carburetor and 240 net horsepower.*

1972 Hurst/Olds. *After a pace car accident in 1971, the big automakers shied away from supplying '72 Indy 500 Pace Cars. Hurst stepped up and built a white-and-gold Hurst/Olds to take to the "Brickyard." A replica package was offered for Cutlass coupes and convertibles. It included a 270-horsepower 455-cubic-inch engine or 300-horsepower W-30 Force-Air engine. Only 629 were built.*

1972 Lincoln Mark IV. *This car was a wild expression of luxury in an automobile. It grew four inches longer than the massive Mark III and a new roof design had oval-shaped opera windows. A 460-cubic-inch V-8 with just 224 (net) horsepower was under its stretched hood. It sold for $8,640 and weighed nearly 5,000 pounds. Production hit 48,591. It also got wildly low miles per gallon figures.*

Big, strong and stylish.
This is the way it's going to be.

Looks like a whole lot of designers got caught looking. Again.

While they were building their traditional "big cars", we were building the most luxurious Pontiac Bonneville ever. (So luxurious our upholstery has been attacked as unfair competition.)

We were also proving, once and for all, that being big is no excuse for being clumsy. With a new 455 V-8, firm suspension, Wide-Track stance.

Now, isn't that the way you want luxury to be? It is. At your Pontiac dealer's.

⩔ Pontiac's new Bonneville

The Wide-Track Family for '70: Grand Prix, Bonneville, Executive, Catalina, GTO, LeMans Sport, LeMans, Tempest and Firebird. Pontiac Motor Division.

(We take the fun of driving seriously.)

The year 1973 would bring America its first gasoline shortage since the World War II rationing of fuel for national defense. Detroit had no hint of what was about to happen in 1970, when this Pontiac advertisement focused on the 455 cubic-inch V-8 under the hood of the Bonneville hardtop.

1973-1982
The Age of Reason

In a sense, the gradual demise of the convertible after 1972 and its revival in 1982 symbolizes the ninth decade of the American automobile. This was a period in which the domestic car changed gradually from a gas-guzzling gargantuan into a thinking man's machine. A combination of social consciousness, Japanese competition and OPEC oil embargoes pressured Detroit into virtually reinventing the automobile. Change came shakily and was somewhat half-hearted at first. Cumbersome crash-bumpers, not-so-efficient emission controls and a short-lived seat belt interlock system caused as many problems as they solved. Then, a second gas crunch in 1979 solidified the industry's resolve towards self-improvement. By 1982, it was apparent that this age of reaction and reason had resulted in the rebirth of American leadership in automotive design and engineering.

1973 Pontiac Grand Am. *A European flavor was promised to buyers of the original Grand Am. However, it was really very American in concept, except for offering bucket seats in four-door sedan models. A very distinctive urethane nose with six vertical slots and a pointed hood made it look unique.*

1973 Mustang Convertible. *Mustang's last convertible of the '70s was attractive and affordable. A six cost $3,102 and a V-8 was just $87 more. This was also the last of the "big" Mustangs with 194 inches of length. After 11,853 were built, the Mustang ragtop became a temporarily extinct species.*

1973 Pontiac Trans AM SD-455. *Not just a big engine, the optional SD-455 was a Super-Duty, low-compression, high-performance V-8. It evolved from sports car racing and made the Trans Am SD-455 America's hottest car. Only 252 of the hot cars were built.*

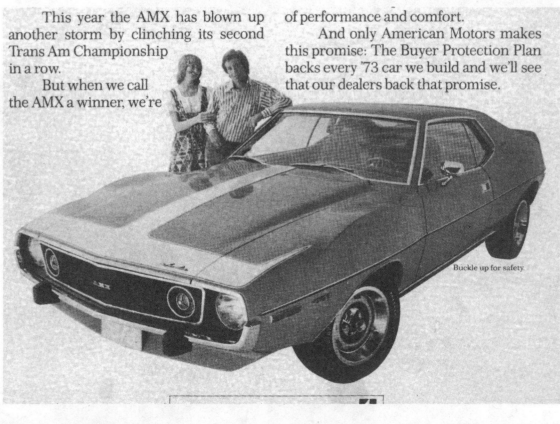

This year the AMX has blown up another storm by clinching its second Trans Am Championship in a row.

But when we call the AMX a winner, we're of performance and comfort.

And only American Motors makes this promise: The Buyer Protection Plan backs every '73 car we build and we'll see that our dealers back that promise.

Buckle up for safety.

1973 Trans-Am Victory Javelin. *Javelins took Trans-Am racing championships in 1971 and 1972. So, the following year AMC offered a "Trans-Am Victory" edition. It had fender decals commemorating the honor, slotted wheels and fat tires. The package helped keep the performance image alive for an extra year.*

1974 Citicar. *Today, many people believe that electric cars are the best answer to America's future transportation needs. The Citicar, built by Florida-based Sebring Vanguard Corporation, is the most successful post World War II electric car ever made from a production standpoint. Power comes from eight batteries.*

1974 Chrysler Imperial Crown. *With a 124-inch wheelbase and 231-inch overall length, this is a car to reckon with in a demolition derby. The Crown Coupe had a half-vinyl top and opera windows. It was priced at $7,356 and only a mere 57 buyers purchased one making survivors very collectible.*

1974 Dodge Challenger. *Making its final appearance as a real pony car, the Challenger was available as a coupe-only for 1974. A 318-cubic-inch V-8 was standard. There was a Rallye option with strobe-type stripes. Despite an attractive price of $3,143, the Challenger generated only 16,437 orders.*

1974 Corvette LS-4. *The Corvette lost its shiny chrome rear bumper. Taking its place was a sloping rear end with a body-color urethane bumper. Big-block V-8s had their final fling this year. The LS-4 option gave you a 454-cubic-inch 270-horsepower engine. A convertible remained in the line and just 5,472 were built. Production of coupes climbed to 32,029.*

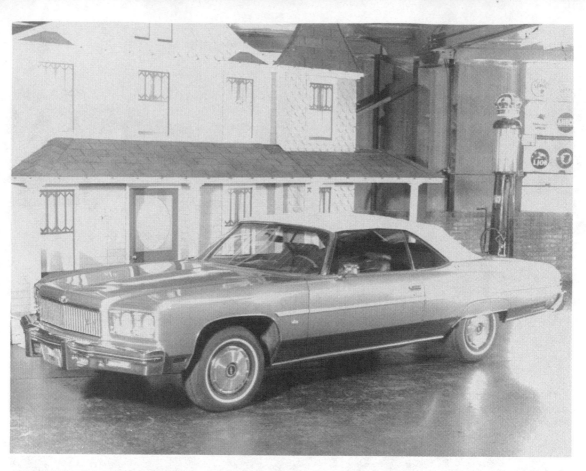

1975 Chevrolet Caprice Classic. *A High-Energy-Ignition system and catalytic converter were new features on Chevrolet's last really full-sized convertible. This Caprice was a big 223 inches long and cost $5,075 up. Its total production was just 8,349 units. A special grille gave the Caprice Classic a touch of class.*

1975 Chevrolet Cosworth Vega. *Cosworth Engineering, of England, gave the four-cylinder Vega engine the high-tech treatment. Modifications included a 16-valve aluminum head, magna-fluxed connecting rods and computerized ignition to extract 120 horsepower from 122 cubic inches. 0-to-60 took only 8.7 seconds. The price tag was $5,416, just a tad less than a new Corvette.*

1975 Chrysler Cordoba. *An opulent-looking new model in the 1975 Chrysler lineup was the Cordoba. It was a specialty coupe that nailed down 60 percent of the company's business. V-8 engines up to 400 cubic-inches were available. Base-priced at $5,581, the Cordoba found over 150,000 buyers.*

1975 Buick LeSabre "Indy 500" Convertible. *A Buick Century Custom Coupe with T-tops and wild graphics was the year's Indy 500 Pace Car. However, 40 special LeSabre convertibles were produced for use in events held during April and May in connection with the main event. The cars were all-white with white notchback seats. They were delivered directly to the 500 Festival Committee. Survivors would be hard to find, since they are rarer than Pace Car replicas.*

1976 AMC Pacer. *Before it played a supporting role in the film "Wayne's World," the poor little AMC bubble-car took its share of ribbing. The Pacer was introduced March 1, 1975 as the first wide, small car. It had many unique design features, such as a larger door on the passenger side. What it did not have was the Wankel engine and front-wheel-drive originally planned.*

1976 Buick Pace Car. *This was Buick's second year in a row as the Indy Pace Car. It was a Century T-top coupe with a turbocharged 231-cubic-inch engine and three times the normal horsepower. This was the first V-6 to pace the 500-mile race. A total of 1,290 cars wearing the gray, black and orange Pace Car package were sold.*

1976 Cadillac El Dorado. *This was the biggest front-wheel drive car in the world and received big play in the media for being the "last" Cadillac convertible. A total of 14,000 were made. The final 200 had special all-white paint with red and blue "bicentennial" accents. They were touted as a good investment and sold at over-sticker prices. Both the high cost and the "last ragtop" claim proved unwarranted.*

1976 Pontiac Trans Am. *The gold-trimmed, black Trans Am Special Edition was custom-converted by Hurst Corporation to create a more glamorous image for the performance Firebird. It was a 50th anniversary model, marking a half-century of Pontiacs. Only 2,590 were made. Hurst hatch roofs went on 643 and only 429 had a big 455-cubic-inch V-8.*

1977 AMC/AMX Hornet. In 1977, American Motors started a three-year effort to generate added sales by reviving the AMX name as a Hornet option. Priced at $799, the AMX package included wheel flares, bright paint, window louvers and a large hood decal. Total production of Hornets was 77,843, but few were AMXs.

1977 Oldsmobile Delta 88. To promote a total redesign of the Delta 88, Oldsmobile supplied the 1977 Indy 500 Pace Car. It was a special T-top coupe with custom graphics. Oldsmobile released the RPO-W44 Pace Car Replica package for $914. A total of 2,401 Delta Royale coupes were equipped with this option.

1977 Dodge Aspen R/T. *Dodge's R/T (road and track) package for the Aspen was essentially an option with bold body graphics, styled wheels and fat white-letter tires. However, when equipped with the extra-cost 360-cubic-inch V-8, the lightweight coupe could fly. There was a Super Pak edition that added front and rear spoilers, special tape stripes, R/T insignias and louvered quarter windows.*

1977 AMC Matador X-2. *American Motors devised the rare X-2 package to make the Matador competitive in stock car racing. It featured below-the-headlamps lower body extensions to smooth out air flow. A modified 1975 style grille was used. It had the end sections cut off and the center section turned upside down. According to stock car driver Bobby Allison, after NASCAR refused to approve the X-2 kit, he obtained some and put them on a limited number of cars that were sold to the public, making a great "American" collector car.*

1978 Mustang King Cobra. *The new-for-1978 Mustang King Cobra was a $1,253 option for the hatch back. In addition to the regular Cobra performance goodies, it had an attention-getting striping and lettering package. Also standard was a 302-cubic-inch V-8, four-speed transmission and power steering and brakes. The package was offered just one year and about 500 were built.*

1978 Corvette Pace Car. *This was Chevrolet's fifth Indy Pace Car, but the first Corvette to have the honor. It was the marque's 25th birthday. The limited-edition model had black paint with "hot" metallic silver accents and red striping. A special dash plaque identified the $13,653 Pace Car. A total of 6,502 were built.*

1978 Chrysler LeBaron Town & Country. *The large Chrysler Town & Country wagons were replaced by an all-new LeBaron version to carry on the famous nameplate. Simulated woodgrain side trim paid homage to the original woodies in the T & C series. The six-cylinder model was $5,672 and the V-8 was $5,848. In all, 21,504 were built.*

1978 Dodge Magnum. *Dodge hoped to recapture the excitement of the original Charger by giving the Magnum XE a distinctive appearance. The keynotes of the design were a horizontally-slotted grille and glass-shrouded headlamps that created an aggressive, functional image. It was offered with 318-, 360- and 400-cubic-inch V-8s, heavy-duty suspension and special dash trim for $5,448. 47,827 were built.*

1979 Hurst/Olds. *This was the seventh Hurst/Olds and 2,499 were created. Cameo white-and-gold finish was used on 1,165 of them. The rest were black-and-gold. T-tops were ordered for 537. Features of the W-30 included a gold grille, gold tapered roof pillars and gold aluminum Sport wheels. Based on the Calais coupe, the Hurst package cost $2,054. The engine was a 350-cubic-inch 170 horsepower V-8.*

1979 Pontiac Trans Am 10th Anniversary. *The 10th anniversary model was a highly-optioned, limited-production car with special silver-and-charcoal color scheme, hatch roof, turbo wheels and a long list of goodies. The only extra was a 403-cubic-inch V-8 used with Turbo-Hydramatic or cruise control. It went into 5,683 cars. The other 1,817 had a 400-cubic-inch V-8 and four-speed manual transmission. This model was the Daytona 500 Pace Car and a decal kit was available.*

1979 Ford Mustang Pace Car. *Highlighting a new body, Ford got the nod to create the year's Indy 500 Pace Car. The new pony car was based on the Fairmont and came in fastback and notch back styles. A design team headed by Jack Telnack turned out this winner. The Pace Car had the 5.0-liter V-8, silver paint with black accents and multi-color decals.*

1979 Lincoln MarK V Bill Blass Designer Series. *A collector's series took the place of the Golden Jubilee edition Lincoln in 1979. The most popular collector version seems to be the dark blue and white "Bill Blass" coupe with its simulated convertible top. This option was about $2,905 extra. Also offered on the Designer Series option list were Cartier, Pucci and Givenchy models.*

1980 McLaren Mustang. *In September 1980 Ford formed a Special Vehicle Operations (SVO) department under Michael Kranefuss, former director of the European competition program. Later in the year, the McLaren model appeared. Features included a grille-less front end, spoilers, functional hood scoops, flared fenders, heavy-duty suspension and turbo-four engine that generated 175 horsepower. Priced at $25,000, the hand-constructed McLarens accounted for just 250 sales.*

1980 Pontiac Turbo-Trans Am Pace Car. *Incorrectly hailed as the first turbocharged American car, the 1980 Indy-pacing Turbo-Trans Am is still very collectible. The $11,195 fully-loaded Pontiac came with special white and gray two-tone paint, white turbo-cast wheels, Oyster white and black upholstery and a 4.9-liter V-8 with an AiResearch turbo that developed 210 net horsepower. It had a 0-to-60 time of 5.2 seconds and top speed of 116 miles per hour. About 5,700 were built.*

1980 AMC Eagle. *The 4x4 Eagle is catching on with collectors as an interesting car. It was introduced in 1980 as an AMC Concord-based model. Coupes, sedans and wagons were offered. All used an advanced four-wheel-drive system. A special Eagle Limited model with power windows, a parcel shelf, fancy carpets, premium door trim, reclining seats and a wood-trimmed steering wheel was $400 extra.*

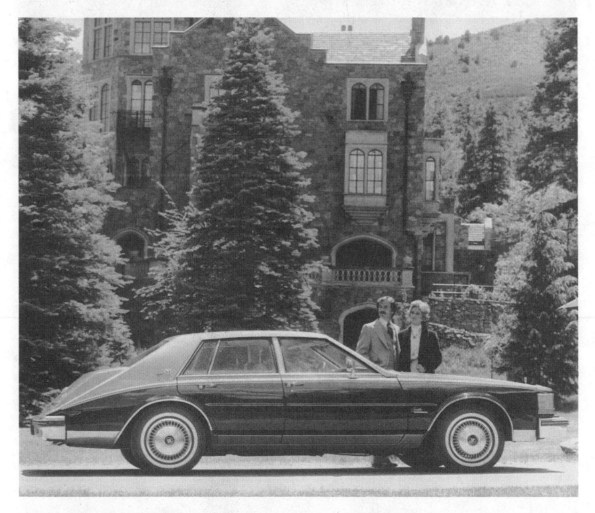

1980 Cadillac Seville Elegante. *Cadillac billed its new-for-1980 Seville as "quite possibly the most distinctive car in the world today and the most advanced." It had a dramatic new shape with a bustle-back body created by designer Wayne Cady under Bill Mitchell's guidance. The look was that of a custom-bodied Rolls-Royce. The Elegante option added $2,934 to the base price of $19,662. A total of 39,344 first-year models were made.*

1981 Buick Indy Pace Car. *The Official Pace Car for the 65th Indy 500 race was a V-6 powered T-top coupe from Buick. It was based on the Regal Sport Coupe, with a special 4.1-liter turbo V-6 that produced 281 horsepower compared to the 125 horsepower of the stock V-6 used in larger Buicks (but, not yet in Regals). The 23 millionth Buick of all time was built in 1981.*

1981 Chrysler Imperial. *The styling of this Cordoba-based Imperial was characterized by an attractive shovel-nose and a bustle-back reminiscent of a 1930s classic. It was big and luxurious, with a 318-cubic-inch 140-horsepower V-8. No-cost options included Mark Cross cloth or leather interiors, digital instruments and clear coat paint. The only extra-cost option for the $18,311 Imperial was a $1,044 power moon roof. Sales came to 7,225 cars, including 148 "Frank Sinatra" editions.*

1981 Delorean DMC-12. *A sleek, sophisticated sports/luxury car with a stainless steel-clad plastic body, the controversial Delorean was one man's expression of the ultimate in elite automobiles. The gull-wing coupe had a $25,000 price tag, 130 miles per hour top speed and supposed 50,000-mile warranty. Priced at $26,175, the American-designed, built-in-Ireland exoticar found only about 4,000 customers.*

1981 Excalibur Series IV. *The new Series IV Excalibur phaeton was introduced in 1981 with a $43,500 price tag ($15,000 higher than the previous model). A Chevrolet 305-cubic-inch 155-horsepower V-8 drove through a Turbo-Hydramatic transmission. A much larger wheelbase was featured. Only 235 examples were constructed in 1981.*

1982 Chevrolet Camaro. *The Z28 was selected as the Indy 500 Pace Car in 1982. Features of the "Indy 500 Commemorative Edition" replicas included Sport mirrors, a rear spoiler, instrumentation, a leather-wrapped steering wheel and a stock-block 5.0-liter V-8 with a choice of Cross-Fire fuel injection (165 horsepower) or four-barrel carburetor (140 horsepower). The cars had silver metallic paint with bright blue metallic accents, blue and red decal stripes, and Indy 500 decals and dash plaques. Only 6,360 of the $10,999 models were made.*

1982 Corvette Collector Edition. *After Corvette production was moved from St. Louis to Bowling Green, Kentucky, plans for an all-new 1983 model were made. Chevrolet released the Collector Edition to mark the milestones. It had silver and gold clear coat paint, special 1967-style wheels, lots of options and a unique opening rear window. This was the first Corvette to sell for over $20,000 ($22,538). Total 1982 Corvette production was 25,407 and about 30 percent were Collector Editions.*

1982 Ford Mustang 5.0-Liter. *"The Boss is Back" said ads for the new 1982 Mustang GT. The backbone of this high-performance model was a 5.0-liter H.O. V-8 with 157 horsepower. It could do 0-to-60 in eight seconds. The body sported monotone front and rear fascias, a color-keyed integral spoiler, body-color cowl grilles and GT badges. The GT sold for $8,308 and 23,447 were manufactured.*

1982 Chrysler LeBaron Convertible. *A revival of interest in ragtops was sparked by Chrysler's 1982 decision to re-enter the market with open-bodied versions of its K-car modified by Cars & Concepts company. The LeBaron was named after the famous coach building firm. For a few extra dollars, the Mark Cross edition was available with leather trim and air conditioning. Chrysler sold 3,045 LeBarons at $11,698 and 9,780 of the Mark Cross models priced at $13,998.*

The Oldsmobile Toronado does more than stand out. It stands alone.

Toronado.

With this personal luxury car, the emphasis is on personal. That's the Olds point of view behind the new 1983 Toronado. So distinctive a look, it looks like nothing else. Another distinction — front-wheel drive. Oldsmobile was the first contemporary U.S. auto company to introduce it, back in 1966. A welcome bit of engineering when the roads turn snowy and slick. Welcome, too, is the news that air conditioning, tilt steering wheel, and cruise control are all standard, along with a traditionally rich interior. Olds Toronado. For you. And you alone.

Oldsmobile

Have one built for you.

By 1983, American cars were beginning to get sporty and exciting again. The industry was learning how to build world-class vehicles that combined eye appeal and power with safety and fuel efficiency. Convertibles were beginning to re-emerge, high-performance cars were back on the market, and personal luxury cars were hot in the marketplace. This advertisement for the Oldsmobile Toronado stresses its distinctive looks, front-wheel-drive technology, long list of convenience options and rich interior appointments.

1983-1993
A Parade of Progress

The 10th decade of the American automobile was an endless parade of progress. First came cars that pumped the excitement level up again: Camaros, Firebirds, T-birds and 5.0-liter Mustangs, not to mention a new generation of convertibles. They looked good and went fast. Next came a period of higher technology, as fuel-injection, turbos, superchargers and active suspensions began to show up on car after car. This was followed by the return of real innovations, such as two-seaters, mid-engined cars and multi-valve engines. The last part of the parade brought along new levels of quality manufacturing to catch up to, and ultimately surpass, the high standards of Japanese automakers. By the end of the decade, the American automobile had climbed back to true greatness.

With 1993 starting the second century of U.S. automotive history, collectors of American cars look forward to another hundred years of motoring excitement. As the past has proven again and again, the domestic automobile has the ability to adapt to a changing world and meet the challenges of the future.

1983 Ford Thunderbird. *The 10th generation T-bird was the smallest since the original two-seater. It had an eye-catching aerodynamic body, an egg crate grille and wraparound headlamps. Immediately popular, the redesign boosted sales from 45,000 the previous year to 122,000. Power came from four- and six-cylinder engines, plus a turbo-four available in an under-$12,000 Turbo Coupe designed for the sports car set. The top-of-the-line Heritage Coupe with a V-8 was $12,516.*

1983 Buick Riviera XX Anniversary. *The Riviera's 20th birthday was celebrated with a convertible that paced the 67th running of the Indy 500. Finished in cream with chocolate brown accents, the XX Anniversary model featured leather seats and real wood trim. A twin-turbo version of Buick's 4.1-liter V-6 producing 350 horsepower was in the actual Pace Car. Production models with the Pace Car package had either a 180-horsepower turbo V-6 or 140-horsepower V-8. Buick built only 1,750 of the new Riviera convertible. Only 128 had a V-6.*

1983 Chrysler Executive Limousine. Chrysler's front-wheel-drive K-car proved very adaptable to conversion work. In late 1983, the company introduced a seven-passenger limousine version selling for $21,900. It offered folding jump seats and an electric division window. These LeBaron-based cars had a 131-inch stance and were Chrysler's first limos in 13 years. Only two were made in 1983. Production grew to 594 in 1984, 759 in 1985 and 138 in 1986, the model's final year.

1983 Hurst/Olds. This was the eighth Hurst/Olds, but it marked the 15th year since the first 1968 model. A unique "lightning rod" Hurst shifter and high-performance 307-cubic-inch V-8 with 180-horsepower were featured. The body was done in black with a silver lower perimeter and red accent striping and decals. A power bulge hood and rear deck lid spoiler were included. Original plans called for 2,500 cars, but this was upped to 3,000. The 1983 Hurst/Olds could go from 0-to-60 miles per hour in around 8.5 seconds.

1984 Ford Mustang SVO. *Ford's Special Vehicle Operations created this sophisticated turbocharged grand touring car with a European flavor. The engine was a 2.3-liter inter-cooled four that produced 175 horsepower and 7.5 second 0-to-60 times. Top speed was around 135 miles per hour. A deep front air dam, functional hood scoop and "bi-plane" rear spoiler added special looks to the $15,596 sports car. The model generated just 4,508 sales its first year.*

1984 Buick Regal Grand National. *This model was built to emphasize the idea that Buicks could be exciting and fun-to-drive cars. It was introduced at the Grand National stock car race at Daytona Beach, Florida. Only 215 were built. When it returned in 1984, it had a sinister looking all black body and 3.8-liter sequential-fuel-injected V-6 that developed 200 horsepower at 4000 rpm. Other features included heavy-duty suspension, air dams, spoilers and special identification badges. Only 2,000 of the 1984 editions were produced.*

1984 Pontiac Fiero Indy Pace Car. *During its introductory year, the two-seat, mid-engined Fiero was selected to pace the Indy 500. Pontiac built three actual Pace Cars with over-the-roof air scoops and 2.7-liter Super-Duty four-cylinder engines of 232 horsepower. A total of 41 replicas were given to Speedway officials. In April, Pontiac started selling replicas to the public. They included white paint, gray lower accents, red stripes, an aero package, slate gray leather seats and decals. The engine was Pontiac's standard "Iron Duke" four with special detailing and a dual outlet exhaust system. The Pace Car package cost $2,895. An estimated 2,185 replicas were made.*

1984 Hurst/Olds. *For the first time since 1968, the Hurst/Olds was silver with black trim and red accents. The new edition was based on the Cutlass Calais, with a hot 307-cubic-inch 180-horsepower V-8. It could do the quarter mile in 16 seconds at 83 miles per hour. Included again was a four-speed automatic with Hurst "Lightning Rod" shifters. As in 1983, the cars came with a large hood scoop, a rear deck lid spoiler, 15-inch Rallye wheels (painted Argent silver) and Hurst/Olds fender decals. About 3,500 were manufactured.*

1985 Dodge Shelby Turbo Charger. The Shelby Charger was the top-performing version of Dodge's small-est model and a turbo was new for 1985. With it, the 136-cubic-inch four was good for 146 horsepower at 5,200 rpm. Turbo lettering decorated the power bulge hood on the $9,553 Shelby, which scaled in at only 2,350 pounds. Electronic fuel injection and a close-ratio five-speed transaxle were standard. Production of this model reached just 7,709 units.

1985 Mustang SVO. In mid-1985, the SVO Mustang received flush-mounted aerodynamic headlamps and turbo improvements that boosted horsepower to 205. MOTOR TREND called the SVO "the best street machine the factory has ever produced" and said it could outrun a Datsun 280 ZX and out handle a Ferrari 308 or Por-sche 944. The price dropped slightly to $14,521, but sales also fell to 1,954. In 1986, the SVO continued with a $15,272 price and sold 3,382 units.

1985 Oldsmobile Indy Pace Car. *Introduced for 1985, the Oldsmobile Calais was aimed at a niche between the Firenza and the Cutlass. The small front-drive car was sporty and contemporary, so a special convertible version was whipped up for Indy 500 Pace Car duties. A total of 2,998 Indy 500 replica packages were then installed on base coupes. This option went for a hefty $1,595.*

1985 Chevrolet Camaro IROC-Z. *The International Race of Champions series gave the IROC option for the Camaro Z28 its name. It began in 1973 with 15 identical Porsches competing. The next year, a switch to Camaros was made. Due to its high media exposure, the series put the Camaro in the limelight. Racing halted in 1980, but started again in 1984. The first production IROC model appeared in 1985. The option sold for $695 and 21,177 cars got it.*

1986-1/2 Pontiac Grand Prix 2+2. *Unfavorable aerodynamics cost Pontiac stock car wins and inspired this car. Its fastback rear window had to appear on a minimum number of production cars to qualify it for racing. Also featured were a silver-and-gray paint scheme with red accents, special front fascia, styled wheels and loads of options. It was $17,800 with a 350-cubic-inch 165-horsepower V-8. About 200 were built.*

1986 Avanti II Convertible. *Avanti Motor Car Company, of South Bend, Indiana was ready to cash in its chips by 1985. President Steve Blake, who made a heroic effort to perpetuate the car, resigned in February. On April 30, 1986, Michael Kelly purchased rights and assets of Avanti and reformed it as New Avanti Motor Car Corporation. He immediately set to work on new models. One was a convertible. By August of that year, early versions of the ragtop were seen in shipment. The classic Avanti made quite a handsome ragtop.*

1986 Corvette Indy Pace Car. *Chevrolet reintroduced the Corvette convertible in 1986 and supplied the Indy Pace Car. The company said all Corvette ragtops should be considered Pace Car replicas. The actual Pace Cars were bright yellow with black Indy 500 decals. All of the cars had the same 5.7-liter TPI (Tuned-Port-Injected) V-8 with aluminum heads, a four-speed overdrive automatic transmission, Gatorback tires on 9.5-inch cast alloy wheels and Bosch anti-lock brakes. Only 7,315 were made.*

1986 Lincoln Mark VII LSC. *The 1986 Lincoln Mark VII LSC was powered by a greatly improved 5.0-liter High-Output V-8 fitted with sequential multi-port fuel injection and stopped by an advanced anti-lock braking system. The Electronic Air Suspension provided the optimum balance between all-out performance and riding comfort. It's also a rare model. Total production of Mark VIIs was 20,056 and only a fraction were $23,857 LSC editions.*

1987 Cadillac Allante. *The LTS (Luxury Two Seater) concept of 1982 evolved into the Allante, a $54,700 convertible with Pininfarina styling on a special 99.4-inch wheelbase. Bodies were built in Italy and flown to Detroit. A 4.1-liter aluminum block V-8 with multiport fuel injection produced 120 horsepower. The Allante was the costliest car ever offered by a U.S. automaker. All 1987 models came with removable hardtops. Only 3,366 were manufactured.*

1987 Buick GNX. *The Buick GNX was a super version of the Regal Grand National built to honor its passing. McLaren Engines, Incorporated got the job of developing a special high-tech, turbocharged V-6 with an intercooler, fuel injection and electronic controls. It gave 276 horsepower at 4,400 rpm. The performance-modified suspension featured a longitudinal torque box. Exterior features included black paint, a power bulge hood, functional cowl vents, GNX badging and a rear spoiler. The GNX listed for $29,290 and total production was 547 cars.*

1987 Ford Thunderbird Turbo Coupe. *The regular T-bird was unchanged, but the Turbo Coupe was significantly revised to provide a road car with leading edge technology. It had many new SVO performance goodies including an intercooler and more efficient IHI turbo. Other features included automatic ride control, ABS brakes, a limited-slip differential, 16-inch VR60 tires, an octane switch and dual exhausts. The $13,028 model boasted 190 horsepower. It had functional hood ducts and Turbo Coupe fender badges. It was picked as the MOTOR TREND "Car of the Year."*

1987 Chrysler LeBaron Convertible. *A new LeBaron convertible appeared to rave reviews. The front-drive luxo-car competed with the T-bird and Olds Cutlass for sales. This was a new market niche for Chrysler. Prices were in the $13,000 range. The ragtop was the first late-model Chrysler designed and constructed as a ragtop. It came out in midyear. A turbo was optional.*

1988 Buick Reatta. *Buick's luxury two-passenger car began production in January 1988. The aerodynamic Sports Coupe was built on a 98.5-inch wheelbase. It had front-wheel drive, a 3.8-liter 165-horsepower V-6, fully-independent suspension and fast-ratio power steering. The $25,000 price included air conditioning, a stereo cassette player, fog lamps, power bucket seats, power windows and locks and a stainless steel exhaust system. Only 4,708 Reattas were made in the first year.*

1988 Shelby CSX-T. *This hot Dodge Shadow-based rocket cost $34.95 ... per day. That's because the 1988 Shelby CSX-T was manufactured exclusively for Thrifty Car Rental Company. "Launch yourself into a white-hot world of turbocharged excitement with the new Shelby CSX-T from Carroll Shelby, the legendary American who's beating the European sports cars at their own high-performance game," said one Thrifty ad. Some people rented the cars to go rallying.*

1988 Hurst/Olds. *Hurst Special Vehicles Group developed the 20th Anniversary Aero Commemorative package to mark the second decade of the Hurst/Olds. "Twenty years ago, it all began when Doc Watson built a one of a kind 455-cubic-inch Cutlass for George Hurst ... and a legend was born," a press kit said. The $1,500 aero kit was actually offered to "assist Oldsmobile dealers in selling the remaining inventory of rear-wheel-drive Cutlasses.*

1988 Pontiac Grand Prix SE. *MOTOR TREND had a hard job picking its "Car of the Year" in 1988, a reflection of the improving quality of American automobiles. The all-new Grand Prix SE won out over five other models. This stunning image car transferred the Grand Prix name to a front-wheel-drive platform powered by a 130-horsepower 2.8-liter V-6. Pontiac general manager J. Micheal Losh poses here with the magazine's "Golden Calipers" award on the hood of an SE.*

1989 Shelby CSX Road Rocket. *The Shelby CSX was again based on the Dodge Shadow coupe. New was a variable nozzle Turbo IV engine with 175 horsepower at 5,200 rpm. Special features of the car included Gatorback tires, Monroe Formula GP shocks, Shelby coil springs, rear disc brakes, a five-speed Gertag transmission and extra-heavy-duty suspension. Body mods included a full aero package, ram-air hood and Kaminari rear wing. Each car had a Shelby serialized dash plaque. Zero-to-60 performance was in the seven-seconds range. Production of 500 to 1,500 cars was projected by Shelby Automobiles.*

1989 Pontiac 20th Anniversary Trans Am. *This car was built to be collectible. An Indy 500 Pace Car, it also commemorated the 20th year of the Firebird Trans Am. It was the first V-6 Trans Am and the fastest Trans Am ever built. The Buick GNX-type turbo V-6 could push it from 0-to-60 miles per hour in 5.3 seconds. Monotone white paint, special optional decals and a long list of goodies were standard. Only 1,500 were built and a $32,000 price tag kept them from selling out quickly.*

1989 Ford Taurus SHO. *Ford's Taurus was popular and successful from the beginning in 1986. New for 1989 was the SHO high-performance model with a 3.0-liter Yamaha dual overhead cam V-6 with four valves per cylinder. It was linked to a Mazda five-speed transmission. The engine developed 220 horsepower at 6,000 rpm. Also included were a ground effects package, alloy wheels and performance tires. The SHO sold for $19,739. It was capable of 0-to-60 in eight seconds and did the quarter-mile in 16.2 seconds at 90 miles per hour.*

1989 Ford Thunderbird SC. *The T-bird lost a V-8, but gained a supercharged, intercooled V-6 in the limited-edition "Super Coupe." The 3.8-liter (232 cubic inch) power plant generated 210 horsepower at 4,000 rpm. Other features of the $19,823 model were aero body fairings, automatic-adjustable suspension, four-wheel disc brakes, 16-inch performance tires, analog gauges, lumbar seats, fog lamps and a five-speed. It was MOTOR TREND's "Car of the Year."*

1990 Corvette ZR-1. *The long-awaited "King of the Hill" Corvette was an inch longer than other models and had distinctive rectangular taillamps, but its big feature was the LT5 engine that combined race-car-like performance with long-term durability and surprising fuel economy. The 32-valve double overhead cam all-aluminum V-8 gave 4.2-second 0-to-60 times. The first ZR-1 was delivered to Glenn Ross in September 1989. He had waited 14 months for it.*

1990 Lincoln Town Car. *Nick Zeniuk and Glen Lyall developed the 1990 Lincoln Town Car in record time of 41 months, cutting nearly a year off the regular design cycle. It incorporated traditional American luxury car traits (large size, interior roominess and V-8 power) in an updated package. The car was designed to emphasize an image that Cadillac had moved away from. "Now, more than ever, what a luxury car should be," claimed an ad for the $27,000 model.*

1990 Chrysler Imperial. *The hallowed Imperial name lay dormant for seven years before its revival in 1990. Based on the front-wheel-drive Dynasty/New Yorker, it got a five-inch wheelbase stretch, a new 3.3-liter V-6 and an Ultradrive electronically-controlled four-speed automatic transmission. Base priced at $24,495, the small-for-its-class, but big-on-elegance Imperial made an interesting entry in the suddenly hot 1990 luxury car marketplace.*

1990 Cadillac Allante Soft-top. *To make the limited-edition Allante slightly more affordable a ragtop convertible with a $51,550 price tag was added. Also new was a digital dash and Pearl white paint (both free on the hardtop-convertible, but extra cost for the new model). There was a smaller steering wheel, too, plus a new Delco-Bose compact disc player and a Traction-Control suspension system. Total production of both models was just 3,101 cars.*

1991 Buick Park Avenue. *Something old and something new was the theme of this all-new 1991·Buick. The company's sales slid from over a million in 1985 to 566,000 for 1988 spurring new general manager Ed Mertz to look for answers. He turned to higher engineering quality and a re-emphasis of the "American car" image. The 205-inch long Buick was in the $25,000 range.*

1991 Eagle Talon. *The Eagle Talon is an exciting looking car for the money, with prices starting below $17,000 for the collectible Turbo edition. A pure sports car with 190 horsepower at 6,000 rpm and user-friendly four-wheel-drive handling, the Eagle Talon can run the quarter mile in just over 13 seconds and hit 60 miles per hour in below seven seconds. The carburated version looks nearly as good, but lacks the Turbo's collector appeal.*

1991 Dodge Stealth R/T Turbo. *A new generation of Dodge super cars was launched with the Stealth. It had the look of a sophisticated sports car combined with brutal, high-tech performance. With a base price of $29,267, the R/T Turbo included a 24-valve V-6 with aluminum cylinder heads, twin turbos and intercoolers, and four-wheel-drive. The engine produced 300 horsepower at 6,000 rpm, giving the car a 0-to-60 time of 5.08 seconds. Top speed was in the world-class super car category at 161 miles per hour.*

1991 Mercury Capri XR2 Convertible. *This affordable and versatile ragtop had front-wheel drive and 2+2 seating. Base Capris featured an electronically fuel-injected 1.6-liter overhead cam engine with five-speed manual or four-speed automatic transaxle. The XR2 version added a turbocharged version of the 1.6-liter four with the five speed. A removable hardtop was featured on both.*

1992 Dodge Viper. *Dodge targeted the Corvette market when it conceived the Viper show car, likening it to a modern interpretation of the Shelby-American Cobra. It created so much excitement that plans were made to convert it into a $50,000 production car in a record-short three years. The Viper's sensuous roadster body features external exhausts and an integral sport bar. For power, a new V-10 engine was developed. It produces 400 horsepower and 450 pound-feet of torque.*

1992 Buick Roadmaster. *Buick resuscitated its traditional nameplate to identify a highly refined version of the "jelly bean" Chevrolet Caprice. The new Roadmaster wagon was released in 1991, but sedans bowed in 1992. Both Roadmaster and Roadmaster Limited had a more aerodynamic shape than the Caprice and standard features included a driver's side air bag, full analog gauges and 5.7-liter 180-horsepower V-8. They reflected Buick's new "total vehicle focus" philosophy in a large size product.*

1992 Hummer. AM General Corporation, of South Bend, Indiana made 100,000 High Mobility Multi-Purpose Wheeled Vehicles (HMMWVs) for the military since 1985. In 1991, the Gulf War put the "Hummers" in the public spotlight and brought requests for civilian models. They bowed late in 1992. Available were the two-passenger open hardtop ($46,550), four-passenger open canvas top ($48,500), four-passenger hard top ($49,950) and four-passenger wagon ($52,950). Features included full-time four-wheel drive and a 6.2-liter diesel V-8.

1992 Chevrolet Camaro Heritage Edition. The Camaro was introduced to the world during model year 1967. For 1992, Chevrolet issued the optional Heritage Edition package to commemorate the marque's 25th anniversary. Its striped hood and deck recalled the appearance of early Z28 models. The option was available on all Camaros, with a choice of red, white or black exterior colors.

1993 Dodge Viper GTS Concept Vehicle. *The Shelby Cobra of the 1960s inspired the Dodge Viper. When this Viper GTS concept vehicle showed up at the 1993 International Automobile Show in Detroit, Michigan this link was very obvious. Its blue finish and white racing stripes adds even more of a pure Shelby image to the high-performance coupe. Since show cars do get into private hands, this prototype will make a great collector car if it manages to survive.*

1993 Chevrolet Camaro Indy Pace Car. *Chevrolet's all-new fourth-generation Camaro was selected to pace the 77th annual Indy 500, thereby increasing its collector appeal to future generations. In addition to three actual Pace Cars, a limited production run of 645 Camaro Z28 Indy Coupes (625 for the United States and 20 for Canada) is scheduled. Speedway officials will to get 125 cars for official use, with the balance going to Chevy's top Camaro dealers.*

1993 Cadillac Presidential Limousine. *While the last-of-the-series 1993 Allante will be a future collectible, Cadillac's Presidential Limousine is our pick for the year's top rarity. Only three of these are being constructed for the United States Secret Service for use by President Bill Clinton and his family. They have a 167.5-inch wheelbase and 270-inch overall length.*

1993 Lincoln Mark VIII. *With a dramatic shape that CAR and DRIVER attributes to the "George Jetson" school of design, the new Mark VIII has looks distinctive enough to match its world-class hardware. Technical goodies include a computerized air suspension system, four-sensor ABS brakes and a 280-cubic-inch 280-horsepower 32-valve Four-Cam V-8. 0-to-60 takes 6.8 seconds.*

For Collector Car Enthusiasts...

Standard Guide to Military Vehicles, 1940-1965
* Includes jeeps, half-tracks, tanks, and more
* Historical information & technical specifications
* Pricing in 6 grades for collectors & veterans
ONLY $29.95

Standard Guide to American Muscle Cars, 1949-1992
* High performance cars from the late '40s through '92
* Highlights classic muscle cars from the '60s & '70s
* 500 photos, specifications, production information
ONLY $19.95

American Volunteer Fire Trucks
* A pictorial history of the rigs used across America
* Over 500 models are featured in photos & text
* A must for firefighters & fans of these vehicles
ONLY $16.95

American Motors, the Last Independent
* An in-depth historical view of American Motors Corp.
* Fully illustrated & well told by Patrick R. Foster
* Includes Hudson, Nash, Rambler, Jeep and today's cars
ONLY $19.95

The Fabulous '50s - The Cars, The Culture
* A photographic history of the cars we loved in the '50s
* Over 500 automotive photos, advertisements & billboards
* Lively captions depict the cultural trivia of this era
ONLY $14.95

Standard Catalog of 4x4's, 1945-1993
* A comprehensive guide to American four-wheel-drive vehicles
* Includes trucks, vans, sports sedans and sports cars
* Technical specifications, production totals, I.D. numbers
ONLY $24.95

1993 Standard Guide to Cars & Prices, 5th Edition
* 130,000 current values for vehicles built from 1901-1985
* Complete listings of models from America & around the world
* Includes 20 current "Bargain Buys" for under $7,000 each
ONLY $15.95

Standard Catalog of Imported Cars, 1946-1990
* This unique book profiles hundreds of models worldwide
* Complete with technical specifications, histories & photos
* Current values based on the I-to-6 condition scale
ONLY $24.95

Antique Car Wrecks
* Adapted from OLD CARS WEEKLY's "Wreck of the Week" column
* Includes more than 400 photos, 80% previously unpublished
* Driving safety is reinforced by this photographic history
ONLY $14.95

Police Cars: A Photographic History
* An up close and personal look at the cars against crime
* 300 pages of early paddy wagons to I990's Corvette Cops
* A must for historical fans of our men and women in blue
ONLY $14.95

MASTERCARD & VISA CUSTOMERS, CALL TOLL-FREE TO ORDER...
(800) 258-0929
Monday - Friday 6:30 am-8:00 pm, Saturday 8:00 am-2:00 pm Central Standard Time

Catalogs For Car Collectors...

Standard Catalog of American Cars, 1805-1942
* 5,000 auto builders' makes and models from 1805-1942
* 4,500 photos present visual details to help restorers
ONLY $45.00

Standard Catalog of American Cars, 1946-1975
* Presenting more than 1,000 vehicle listings from 1946-1975
* Over 1,500 photographs aid in vehicle identification
ONLY $27.95

Standard Catalog of American Cars, 1976-1986
* Presents thousands of cars manufactured in America
* Helps pinpoint tomorrow's collector cars today
ONLY $19.95

Standard Catalog of American Light-Duty Trucks
* All new 2nd edition presents 500 truck listings, 1896-1986
* ID data, serial numbers, codes, specs, current pricing
ONLY $29.95

Standard Catalog of Ford
* Profiles every Ford make and model built from 1903-1990
* More than 500 photographs aid in identification
* ID data, serial numbers, codes, specs, current pricing
ONLY $19.95

Standard Catalog of Chevrolet
* Profiles every Chevy model manufactured from 1912-1990
* Over 500 photos bring restorers visual aid during projects
* ID data, serial numbers, codes, specs, current pricing
ONLY $19.95

Standard Catalog of Chrysler
* Profiles each Chrysler make and model in detail, from 1924-1990
* Presents I-to-6 conditional pricing through 1983 models
* ID data, serial numbers, codes, specs, production totals
ONLY $19.95

Standard Catalog of Buick
* Profiles every Buick model & make crafted from 1903-1990
* Chassis specs, body types, shipping weights, current pricing
* Fascinating stories, historical perspectives, photo profiles
ONLY $18.95

Standard Catalog of Cadillac
* All the makes that made Cadillac famous, from 1903-1990
* Photographic perspectives, codes, specs, ID and serial numbers
* Includes I-to-6 conditional pricing for current value comparisons
ONLY $18.95

Standard Catalog of American Motors
* Presents every model in the AMC family from 1903-1987
* Hudson, Nash, Metropolitan, Rambler, AMC/Jeep, AMX
* Factory prices, today's values, technical specifications
ONLY $19.95

Standard Guide to Automotive Restoration
* Matt Joseph's technical, hands-on guide for all restorers
* Complete system-by-system instructions for all makes & models
* More than 400 detailed photos aid in correct application
ONLY $24.95

MASTERCARD & VISA CUSTOMERS, CALL TOLL-FREE TO ORDER...
(800) 258-0929
Monday - Friday 6:30 am-8:00 pm, Saturday 8:00 am-2:00 pm Central Standard Time

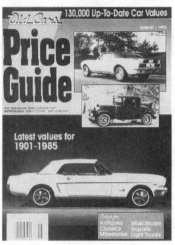